THERESE NEUMANN
Mystic and Stigmatist

*"For I reckon that the sufferings of this time
are not worthy to be compared with the glory to
come, that shall be revealed in us."*
—Romans 8:16-18

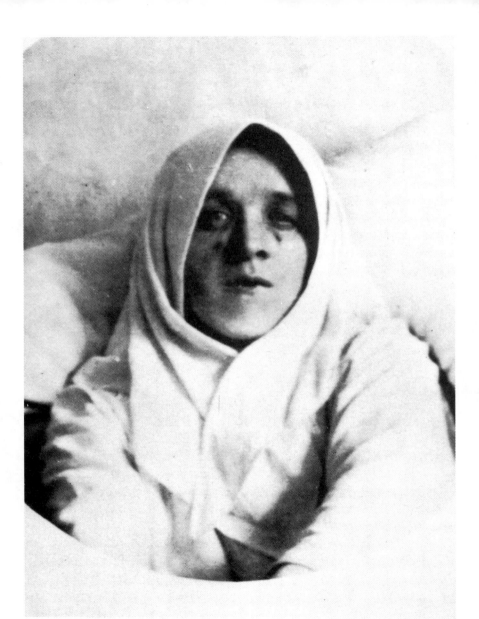

Therese Neumann (1898-1962), mystic and stigmatist from Konnersreuth, Bavaria, West Germany, shown suffering the Passion of Jesus, as she did over 700 times throughout her life.

THERESE NEUMANN
Mystic and Stigmatist
1898—1962

by
Adalbert Albert Vogl

*"But if you partake of the sufferings of Christ,
rejoice that when his glory shall be revealed,
you may also be glad with exceeding joy."*
—1 Peter 4:13

TAN BOOKS AND PUBLISHERS, INC.
Rockford, Illinois 61105

TAN BOOKS AND PUBLISHERS, INC.
P.O. Box 424
Rockford, Illinois 61105
1987

"Always bearing about in our body the mortification of Jesus, that the life also of Jesus may be made manifest in our bodies. . .For that which is at present momentary and light of our tribulation, worketh for us above measure exceedingly an eternal weight of glory."

—2 Corinthians 4:10-17

DIOCESE OF SAN JOSE

November 13, 1987

Mary Frances Lester
Tan Books and Publishers
P. O. Box 424
Rockford, Illinois 61105

Dear Miss Lester:

Bishop DuMaine received the comments from the second reading of
Mr. Vogl's book, <u>Therese Neumann, Mystic and Stigmatist</u>, and has
asked me to respond in his name.

He has decided not to give an <u>Imprimatur</u> for this book. His
decision not to grant this is not because of anything in the book
that is contrary to Faith and morals. His reasons for not grant-
ing it are:

    a. In existing Church Law, the subject of this book is not
        included in the list of those requiring an <u>Imprimatur</u>.

    b. There is a growing practice in the West not to grant an
        <u>Imprimatur</u> unless absolutely required.

I want to emphasize that his decision is not a judgment against
anything that is in the book. It is based solely on the fact that
this type of book does not require an <u>Imprimatur</u>.

Sincerely,

Reverend Terrence J. Sullivan
Vicar General

cc: Bishop Pierre DuMaine

DECLARATION OF OBEDIENCE

In loving obedience to the decrees of several Roman Pontiffs, in particular those of Pope Urban VIII, I declare that I in no way intend to prejudge Holy Mother Church in the matter of saints, sanctity, miracles and so forth. Final authority in such matters rests with the See of Rome, to whose judgment I willingly submit.

—Adalbert Albert Vogl
The Author

CONTENTS

Preface xi

Introduction: How I Came to Write This Book xv

Further Acknowledgments xxiii

1. Therese Neumann's Birth and Early Years 1

2. Therese Receives the Wounds of Christ 7

3. Therese's Suffering of the Passion of Our Lord 11

4. Therese and the Holy Eucharist 17

5. Abstinence from Food and Drink 23

6. Therese Did Not Sleep 26

7. Therese Neumann's Visions 27

8. The Language Phenomenon 48

9. Mystical Recognition of Priests, Relics, the Holy
   Eucharist, and Priestly Blessings 52

10. Cures, Prophecy, Bilocation, and Other Mystical Gifts 56

11. Therese's Daily Activities, Daily Sufferings, and Personality 63

12. Therese Neumann and World War II 70

13. Investigation by the Church 80

14. Conversions 88

15. The Crowds of Visitors 90

16. A Great Privilege Was Ours 93

17. Good Friday of 1951 102

18. The Neumann Family 104

19. Father Naber 105

20. A Seminary for Late Vocations 107

21. The Last Project and Death of Therese Neumann 110

22. The Deaths of Persons Close to Therese Neumann ... 116

23. Visits to Germany in 1973 and 1975—Meetings with
    Five Friends of Therese Neumann 125

24. Critics of Therese Neumann 130
25. Conclusion: The Genuineness of Therese Neumann's
    Mystical Experiences 141
26. Cause for Beatification 151
Appendix: Fr. Ingbert Naab's Open Letter to Hitler 161
Petition for Opening of the Cause for Beatification
    of Therese Neumann 173

PREFACE

We are assured in Scripture that the Church will be identified by miracles, and there has not been a period in history when the promise of her Divine Saviour has not been fulfilled. It has frequently happened that miracles have occurred in great numbers during periods of greatest skepticism— obviously God's answer to man's endeavor to deny or limit His power to deal with the work of His creative hands. It was at the height of the 19th-century rationalism that the miracles of Lourdes confounded the skeptics and the scoffers, and every poisonous "ism" has found an antidote in the miraculous phenomena that have counteracted the poison and revitalized the faith of all who cared to see the truth and its Author behind these preternatural events.

The marvels of stigmatization and inedia (living without the need to eat) have been part of the authentic history of the Church for centuries. That the Divine Saviour should memorialize His redemptive Wounds in the bodies of His saints, or that the Bread of Angels should prove sufficient nourishment for certain of God's elect, should occasion no great wonderment or disquietude among those who believe in God and are aware that there are higher ends and purposes conceivable than the slavish and unrelenting observance of the laws of nature.

Why must it be assumed that God has tied His own hands, the very hands that brought the universe into being? That a pure spirit, whose power is infinite, should be forced to submit to physical laws pertaining to an infinitely lower order of being, and be forever obliged to avoid making exceptions to these laws, is utterly ridiculous. This is the only way that materialistically-minded people are shocked into realization that God has power over matter—matter which they had presumed to be immutable and subject to absolutely inexorable laws. Must we hold that the 20th century is an exception—that the phenomenon which marked Assisi in the thirteenth century is beyond God's power in the twentieth century?

If the devil has any part in this, as has been suggested, it is the first time in history that the house of Beelzebub has been divided against itself—something that our Saviour has said would not happen. During the greater part of the last quarter century, and even longer, hundreds and thousands of people have stood at the bedside of Therese Neumann and returned better Christians, profoundly impressed by the drama of the death of Our Lord. In all Therese's life there is nothing that would make the devil happy.

According to a survey made in the 1920's, the number of people elected chosen by Almighty God to bear the stigmata, the wounds of Our Lord, comes to well over 300. Only recorded and known cases were taken into consideration in this report. Perhaps the most famous instance is that of St. Francis of Assisi, who received the stigmata two years before his death in 1224. It is noteworthy that despite his fame at the time, he tried and almost succeeded in keeping the fact of his stigmatization from becoming known.

Other chosen people mentioned in the report who lived within the last century were: Anne Catherine Emmerich of Germany, who died in 1824; Maria Woerl of Bozen, Austria, who died in 1868; Louise Lateau of Belgium; and St. Gemma Galgani of Italy, who died in 1903. The phenomenon of Louise Lateau is similar to other cases of stigmatization. She bore the wounds of our Saviour on her body for the last 15 years of her life and was sustained solely by the Holy Eucharist for 12 of those years, until her death at the age of 33.

In the twentieth century the two most famous stigmatists are Padre Pio of Pietrelcina, Italy, who bore the wounds of Christ from 1918 until his death in 1968, and Therese Neumann, who bore the stigmata from 1926 until her death in 1968. In both cases this mystical gift from God strengthened the faith of many, many people and showed the spiritual value of suffering in God's plan. Through this book may many more people come to know about the life of Therese Neumann, mystic and stigmatist.

INTRODUCTION
How I Came to Write This Book

Ever since the unusual manifestations in Konnersreuth, Bavaria, Germany, made headlines all over the world in 1926, there has been an ever-increasing desire for information about the mystic, Therese Neumann.

It was in the summer of 1927 that I first met Therese; realizing the significance of her life, a flame was kindled in my heart and has grown in intensity as the years pass by. In many of my lectures I have tried to share with my listeners the knowledge of Therese Neumann that I have gained during the past 49 years. From the very beginning to the present day, I have been fully convinced of the fact that the manifestations in Konnersreuth are a gift from God to all of us through the person of Therese Neumann. I feel, therefore, that the matter is not a mere sensation, but rather a message to us from our Creator for our spiritual enlightenment.

In addition to the many hours I have spent with Therese, the Neumann family and Father Naber over a period of more than 40 years, I have had the extraordinary experience of discussing Konnersreuth with many Church dignitaries, medical doctors and prominent lay people of reputation and integrity, all of whom were in close association with the mystic.

The three people who have contributed most to my knowledge of Therese Neumann are my priest uncles: Rt. Rev. Msgr. Adalbert Vogl, Rt. Rev. Msgr. Karl Vogl and Rev. Prof. Sebastian Vogl, who were near and dear to me, and who also had the privilege of being close friends of Therese Neumann from the beginning of her mystical life. Therese was particularly close to Msgr. Adalbert Vogl.

All that I have written about Therese Neumann comes either directly from her personally or from Father Naber, Mr.

Neumann (her father), her brother August, her sisters Ottilie and Marie, or from many other people who knew her personally. Many are mentioned, but more have been omitted. Altogether, I have interviewed an untold number of people over a span of roughly forty years. My standards have been set very high; as mentioned, no one was ever interviewed unless he actually knew Therese personally. Included in this group are: Cardinal Faulhaber of Munich, Archbishop Andreas Rohracher of Salzburg, Abbot Willibald Mangraf (Benedictine) of Vilshofen, and many priests, professors, educators, and lay people of all walks of life. The end result of the hundreds of hours of hard work is included in this book.

Altötting, Bavaria, my birthplace, is a famous pilgrimage center dedicated to the "Lady of Altötting"; the shrine dates back 1200 years. The shrine houses the miraculous statue of Our Lady, which is a center of veneration for nearly a million faithful every year. Here, too, St. Konrad of Parzham lived and died and is buried. Many Altöttingers still living, including my mother, aunt and uncle, knew him well when he (then Brother Konrad) was porter at St. Ann's Capuchin monastery, feeding the poor at the cloister. Among the many thousands of devout pilgrims who gather annually are numerous high ecclesiastical dignitaries, princes of Church and state, and people of all walks of life. Here, too, Therese Neumann and members of her family journeyed often to pray at the shrine. Therese requested Msgr. Adalbert Vogl to offer many Masses on the main altar there. As a choir boy from 1918 to 1923, I very vividly recall singing at Church functions for the former Papal Nuncio to Bavaria, Cardinal Pacelli, later to become Pope Pius XII, as well as for Cardinal Michael von Faulhaber and many other high dignitaries, all of whom were well acquainted with my uncles.

The history of Altötting from 1900 on will undoubtedly mention the names of the three above-mentioned priests who, by their devotion, theological training and appointment by Bishop Felix von Ow, Bishop of Passau, Bavaria, were closely connected with the administration of the holy shrine and all

Church functions associated with it, as well as with the official Catholic paper, *Altöttinger Liebfrauenbote*—the *Messenger of Our Lady of Altötting*, the offices of which were also in Altötting. This weekly publication had as many as 110,000 subscribers all over the German-speaking world; it is still in existence. Uncle Adalbert was administrator of the holy shrine in Altötting for over 30 years, Uncle Karl was founder and chief editor of *Altöttinger Liebfrauenbote* and Uncle Sebastian was Professor of Theology at the diocesan seminary of Passau for 30 years. Uncle Karl was one of the best-known Catholic journalists in Germany, Austria and Switzerland in the years 1910-1935. (This is the same Father Karl Vogl who wrote up the story of the Earling, Iowa exorcism case; this story has been published as a book entitled *Begone Satan*.) He was papal chamberlain, a personal friend of Cardinal Pacelli (later Pope Pius XII).

I may add here that the Vogl family as a whole had been on the black list of the Hitler regime (which came into power in 1933), but my uncles Adalbert and Karl had the sad distinction of being marked by the brutal Gestapo for persecution far beyond the normal well-known Hitler tactics. Uncle Karl was the first to feel the diabolical blows of an unchristian regime. The very next day after Hitler came to power in 1933, the SS stormed his home, ransacked it, and told my uncle he was *"finished"* as of that moment. My uncle was promptly removed from his office and stripped of all authority, put into involuntary retirement, and harassed by the Gestapo day and night; he finally died a natural death in 1938. Had it not been that way, he surely would have found a brutal death in some concentration camp. Uncle Adalbert was similarly kept under the watchful eyes of the infamous Gestapo. The hatred of these henchmen reached a climax just 24 hours before the army of liberation entered Altötting in April, 1945; at that time Msgr. Adalbert Vogl was publicly executed for God and country, with five other prominent citizens, within the shadow of the Holy Chapel of Altötting. (During the last days of the Hitler regime in 1945 at least 100 Catholic priests were executed by the S.S. or S.A. without any kind of trial.)

My thoughts go back to the days when I returned to Altötting in 1927 after spending four happy years with Father Steiger in Earling, Iowa. I was born in Bavaria in 1910, and emigrated to the United States in 1923. Shortly after my return to Bavaria in 1927, my uncle, Msgr. Adalbert Vogl, called me to his office one afternoon in June of that year to meet a very distinguished pilgrim. That day, the day I first saw Therese Neumann and her father and Father Naber, their parish priest, was indeed a very memorable one. I was a very inquisitive young man, 17 years old at the time, and here was a young woman who I'd heard hadn't eaten in five years. I said to myself, "I'd like to see that!" Therese Neumann, who weighed 130 lbs. at the time, didn't eat anything that day. Father Naber teased her about that, and she came right back at him, "I'm eating with my eyes!" She was a very jolly person.

My uncles had visited Therese in Konnersreuth and had been with her during and between ecstasies. The Friday sufferings had left them more convinced than ever that Therese was a person specially chosen by God. Their convictions were shared by numerous other dignitaries of the Church and other learned people with whom they discussed Konnersreuth.

I have always felt fortunate in having had members of my own family who, by their priestly training and objective thinking and the important ecclesiastical positions they held, were able to evaluate the meaning of Konnersreuth far better than the average layman. In addition to their own intellectual opinions, they in turn had the great opportunity to inquire further and to discuss the matter with hundreds of Church leaders—cardinals, bishops, abbots and many distinguished men of the Church and state.

The many pilgrims who came to visit the shrine made Altötting a "nerve center" of German Catholic life. The very pulse of German thinking could be felt there. Through this medium anyone could tell you that the German Catholic world has always believed wholeheartedly in Therese Neumann and the occurrences in Konnersreuth. From the highest ecclesiastical personalities to the most humble Bavarian pilgrim, the person of Therese Neumann has represented something uplifting . . . something holy, something to be considered as a gift from God to man. These people were not shackled with "scientific" doubtings which would prevent them from recognizing and accepting God's miracles in their midst. They had confidence in their priests and the leaders of the Church, and if there ever had been any reason to doubt what happened in Konnersreuth, there would have been hundreds of well-qualified leaders from both the Church and the secular community who would have been the first to come forth with such news and inform the people of the truth.

I was delighted when my uncles met Prof. Wutz, for this afforded us an opportunity to learn firsthand the authenticity of the language phenomenon which Therese experienced during many of her ecstasies. Prof. Wutz, the priestly scholar of the seminary of Eichstätt, Bavaria, was an expert in the Old Testament, Biblical science, and Oriental languages, and contributed immeasurably to our belief in the supernatural origin of the happenings at Konnersreuth. He had been constantly with Therese during many of her ecstasies and was one of the first to be able to translate all of the languages which Therese spoke, including Greek, Aramaic, Latin and Hebrew.

The year 1927 brought us ever closer to the realization that the phenomenal occurrences of Konnersreuth could not be explained by human intellect and should therefore be considered, because of their extraordinary developments, as divinely inspired. Hundreds of worthy priests and lay people who had visited Therese Neumann and who had seen the mystic in her sufferings came to the same conclusion.

The name of Therese Neumann became known all over the world, and it was interesting to follow the many reports about her in the press. The communistic and socialistic publications and others of similar ideologies outdid themselves in attempting to nullify and ridicule Konnersreuth. One day the *Wiener Abend* (*Vienna Evening*), a radical newspaper, was sent to my Uncle Karl. An article on Therese Neumann was illustrated with a cartoon of a poor peasant blindfolded and priests filching money, while the peasant remained ignorant of their deception.

Shortly after that, another paper, the *Saxony Daily Worker*, announced with a front page headline: "Konnersreuth Is Finished." It told of a Silesian coal miner by the name of Paul Diebel who had supposedly received the wound marks of Christ on his body. This man was pictured in front of a circus stand, dressed in a bathing suit, while people were standing in line ready to pay admission to see his "act." Upon investigation no one ever found this Mr. Diebel.

The *Tribune*, a Saxony socialistic newspaper, was not to be outdone. It printed "extra editions" with big headlines: "The Saint of Konnersreuth Exposed," "Her Past," "Courting a Swindler," "The Saint an Illegitimate Child," and "What Is the Answer of the Catholic Church?"

Uncle Karl, with the powerful medium of his paper, *Altöttinger Liebfrauenbote*, published many articles favorable to Therese Neumann and counteracted the slanderous attacks on her good name. Other Catholic publications, such as the *Salzburger Katholische Kirchenzeitung*, the official paper of the Archdiocese of Salzburg, Austria, printed articles by my uncle and informed its readers of the actual facts about Therese Neumann as they became known to him from unimpeachable sources of the utmost reliability. For eight years I used every available opportunity to be at my uncle's side to hear the many discussions about Therese Neumann and to read with eagerness the many articles which came to his desk.

Those who were best informed in the case counteracted the adverse criticism of Therese immediately. The sources from which the most radical opposition against Konnersreuth came were usually of an anti-religious nature, as was discovered upon investigation. It was the opinion of the Catholic clergy and lay people, in great majority, as we found it over a period of many years, that time would nullify the normal opposition to the mystic. This was the general feeling of the hundreds of influential personalities among the clergy and laity alike. Yes, time has been in favor of Therese Neumann.

After years of continuous study of her case, I have never once found the slightest deviation from the precise plan which Our Master has laid down for this soul whom He chose to bear His wounds and to receive many other precious mystical gifts.

It was some time in 1928 when Uncle Karl became acquainted with a well-known colleague in the secular journalistic field, Dr. Fritz Gerlich, editor of Bavaria's largest newspaper, *The Münchener Neueste Nachrichten*. Gerlich was a non-Catholic who belonged to a group of liberals and had not been affiliated with any particular church. He became somewhat startled over the extraordinary news coming out of Konnersreuth. His office had received many reports from my uncle's paper. Gerlich respected my Uncle Karl as a man, as well as for the truthful reporting that had made him famous even beyond Germany's borders.

Soon after their meeting, Gerlich found his way to Konnersreuth to satisfy his growing interest in the case of Therese Neumann. The various facts which he had learned from reading were much too extraordinary for him to believe. Dr. Gerlich spent quite some time in Konnersreuth and made repeated visits there. Father Naber and Therese Neumann afforded him every possibility to see for himself the Friday sufferings and other supernatural occurrences. Gerlich became convinced of the genuineness of the case of Therese Neumann.

A few years after becoming acquainted with her and having learned the deep significance of God's mystics, he joined the Catholic Church and became one of the most famous of the many converts Konnersreuth has produced. His life was completely changed. He wrote two excellent books on Therese. Soon afterwards, he left the *Münchener Neueste Nachrichten* and founded his own paper, which he so rightly called *Der Gerade Weg* (*The Straight Path*). He used his exceptional talents in journalism to combat the evil philosophy of Hitler which was creeping into the minds of the Bavarian people. His paper and that of Uncle Karl were in the front line of the fight against the Hitler tyranny and served as a powerful bulwark to ward off the onrushing tide of neo-paganism. When Hitler came to power in 1933, the same fate that befell my uncles also ended Gerlich's brilliant career all too soon. Dr. Fritz Gerlich was thrown into the Dachau concentration camp, where he died a martyr's death for the cause of God and the country he loved so well.

It has been with some reluctance that I have written the story of these men. However, I wished to acknowledge that I owe my knowledge of Therese Neumann—and more important, my personal acquaintance with Therese, her family and Father Naber—directly to these worthy martyrs.

FURTHER ACKNOWLEDGMENTS

As this book neared completion I became more and more aware of the fact that many, many wonderful people had inspired, helped and given me encouragement in this undertaking of mine, which has lasted over forty years.

My wife, Esther, with whom I have shared many visits with Therese, has been a constant partner in discussing our experiences, keeping a daily journal each evening on the observations we had made during the time we were with the mystic, so that we could recall the details accurately at a later date. Her help was always ready and her mind fresh and inspiring in making comments and suggestions. Her assistance in organizing and technically preparing the manuscript has greatly facilitated the completion of this book.

I also want to show my appreciation to my son Frank and his wife, Terry. With her cooperation Frank was able to make three trips to Bavaria in order to help me with driving the car. We went all over Bavaria to interrogate people, and it was a big help for me to leave the driving to Frank. Today we can still picture Frank as a four-year-old sitting on the lap of Therese Neumann, her arms around him. Thank you, Frank and Terry.

About two years ago, through our group here in San Jose, we met Mrs. Carol Wenzel. She sensed that with the tremendous job at hand she would like to help me whenever possible. She did that. Tapes had to be made, and she saw to it that the right ones were procured; she also saw to it that reprints of pictures were made. My thanks go out to her for the valuable help.

Through Carol Wenzel we met Mary McDonald from San Francisco. She, too, and always without asking, helped me in many ways. The burden of expenses became lighter when she was around. Thank you, Mary, for your help.

Others who have assisted me in gaining later information of Therese were Msgr. Ludwig Uttlinger and his secretary, Miss Lill. The monsignor is a long-time choirmaster of the National Shrine of Altötting. It was his office that introduced me to the Archbishop, Dr. Andreas Rohracher of Salzburg, Austria, now retired in Altötting, Bavaria. This gave me the opportunity, with my wife also present, to have an hour-long interview with this great churchman. He in turn called his friend, the Bishop of Regensburg, Dr. Rudolf Gräber, and arranged an interview for me with Dr. Carl Sträter, S.J., who was the diocesan appointee of the Bishop to conduct the investigative process regarding the case of Therese Neumann as the Vice-Postulator. The deposition I gave to him on my knowledge and experiences with Therese lasted over one and one-half hours.

Impressed by my sincerity and personal knowledge of Therese, Father Sträter later made it possible for me to meet Anni Spiegl of Eichstätt, Bavaria. Anni Spiegl was a long-time friend and confidante of Therese Neumann. I am sorry to say that when I met Anni on September 23, 1975, in the company of Father Sträter, she was on her deathbed. Meeting Anni Spiegl was like finding a long-lost sister who had been a lifelong persistent fighter for the truth and genuineness of Konnersreuth. The kindness, the information and whole spirit that she conveyed to us in a long interview, in spite of her illness, are something I shall never forget and for which I shall be eternally grateful.

THERESE NEUMANN
Mystic and Stigmatist

— *Chapter 1* —

THERESE NEUMANN'S BIRTH AND EARLY YEARS

Therese Neumann was born on Good Friday, April 8, 1898, in the small village of Konnersreuth in northeastern Bavaria, the eldest of ten children. This happens to have been the very year when St. Therese of Lisieux, the Little Flower, who later played such an important part in Therese Neumann's life, passed to her eternal reward. Therese Neumann, however, was named after the "big Therese," that is, St. Teresa of Avila, Spain, a powerful patron before the throne of God. (The German spelling of Therese Neumann's first name is "Theres.") Neither Church nor school records identify little Resl ("Resl" was Therese's nickname) as a person of any unusual attainment. Her grades were just average. It might be said that the one exceptional thing about her was her quiet, unobtrusive piety.

The Neumann family was always in rather meager circumstances, owning a small farm, the earnings of which were supplemented by Mr. Neumann's income as a tailor. It was fortunate that Therese, the eldest child, was sturdy and able to assist her parents in caring for her younger brothers and sisters. Therese's vital role in the rearing of the younger children was especially necessary when her father was called into the service during the First World War. She regarded no task as beyond her strength and was as able as most men to carry on the heavy farm work. She remarked to me that while she did a man's work, she also had a man's appetite. This girl who was later to subsist without food once ate much more than the average man.

1

Therese's ambition was to become a missionary sister, and she was especially hopeful that she would be sent to darkest Africa. She had a special love for the out-of-doors in all its varied beauty. This deep interest was manifest in the variety of plant and bird life which enlivened her little room.

A far-reaching change in her life began, without anyone realizing it, on the fateful Sunday, March 10 of 1918. Fire broke out in the barn of Martin Neumann, Therese's uncle, for whom she was working. As part of a bucket brigade, she was lifting pails of water to someone higher up in the stable. To do this better, she stood on a stool. After sustained exertion, her clothes water-soaked, she became utterly exhausted and fell to the floor. With very severe pains in her spine, and unable to walk alone, she was helped by a woman to reach her home nearby.

The fall had caused partial paralysis of the spine, accompanied by very severe cramps in her legs. Therese was placed under medical care. The efforts of skilled doctors from Waldsassen, Drs. Göbel and Burkhart, were unsuccessful in bringing any relief in her serious condition. She became worse every day. One thought caused Therese great sorrow—she felt that her chances of becoming a missionary sister were fading away.

While resigned to her serious affliction, Therese sought in every way to surmount it and to be as active as her limited strength would permit. These efforts resulted in several additional accidents and injuries. One day she fell from her chair; while prone on the floor, she struggled to get to her feet, but could not do so without help; she found she had been struck almost blind. In her continued efforts to shuffle around, she often fell again. One of her most serious falls was down the basement steps in her home. These falls increased the severity of her painful cramps. Added to all this, fainting spells occurred which often left her unconscious for several days. Medical experts seemed powerless to help Therese or to hold out any hope to her grieving family. This sorrow reached a climax in March, 1919, when Therese became totally blind.

Bedsores caused by her long confinement in this helpless condition added to her great sufferings. Dr. Mittendorfer, of Munich, a medical adviser to Therese Neumann later during her mystical life, told me that these sores were so deep that the bones were exposed. She had such severe nausea that she was forced to live only on liquids.

What a tremendous change had occurred in the life of Therese Neumann! A short while ago she had been a strong and healthy girl, with the ability to work hard; now she found herself a burden to the ones she would so very much like to help. She offered herself up to the Most Sacred Heart of Jesus. Her ability to suffer in the true spirit of submission to the will of God was a reflection of her wonderful religious home life and conformity to the Master. The members of the family took turns reading to her about our Blessed Saviour, His holy Mother, and the saints. The story of the Little Flower of Jesus was one of her favorites.

Father Naber, pastor of the parish of St. Lawrence ("Laurentius") in Konnersreuth since 1909, had been Therese's spiritual director for nine years. He was a most devoted pastor, especially to those most in need of comfort. Therese, perhaps the most afflicted of all the people in Konnersreuth, claimed a large measure of his paternal care and he came to know her, as well as the members of her family. He was especially impressed by the quiet resignation with which she bore her excruciating sufferings.

In 1922 a young seminarian came to visit Therese Neumann. He asked her to pray for him, especially for the relief of a throat condition that threatened the continuance of his studies for the priesthood. Therese agreed to make a novena with him for his recovery. It was Therese's secret wish that she would be able to assume the throat ailment with its attendant suffering in order that the young man would be enabled to continue his priestly studies without this serious affliction. The result of the novena was that the throat trouble was transferred from the seminarian to Therese; she bore this along with her blindness, paralysis, horrible bedsores and protracted fainting spells. For eight years she endured the painful throat ailment and was only relieved of it when the young man, whose priesthood she had thus ensured, was celebrating his first Mass. As he pronounced the words of Consecration, Therese was completely cured of the affliction.

In spite of Therese's poor physical condition, and particularly the lameness and blindness which she had endured for four years, she remained at a very high level of spiritual happiness and contentment by offering these afflictions for the intentions of the crucified Saviour.

A very joyful day was approaching for Therese. Sunday, April 29, 1923 was the day scheduled for the beatification ceremonies in Rome of the Carmelite nun, the saintly Therese of Lisieux, who had promised to let fall from Heaven a "shower of roses." Flowers were arranged to adorn the picture of the nun which Therese had received from her father years ago and which was prominently displayed in her little room. A novena was begun and special prayers were said in spiritual preparation for the day when the Little Flower would be officially numbered among the beatified.

Therese's heart felt joyful as the day approached. Then on Sunday, as the ceremonies at St. Peter's in Rome were drawing to a close, the newly beatified Therese of Lisieux "showered a bouquet of roses" on the devoted sufferer, Therese Neumann, in Konnersreuth; at the instant of beatification, Therese found that her eyesight was completely restored.

On May 17, 1925, when Therese of Lisieux was canonized and became officially recognized as a saint of the Catholic Church, Therese Neumann heard her voice. Softly and distinctly, the saint said to her, *"Resl, willst du nicht gesund werden?"* (Therese, do you not want to become well?) Therese Neumann answered, *"Alles ist mir recht. Gesundwerden, krankbleiben, sterben, wie es Gott will."* (Anything is all right with me: to be healthy, to remain sick, to die, whatever is the will of God.) The voice continued, *"Resl, macht es dir keine Freude, wenn du eine Erleichterung im Leiden bekämst, wenn du wenigstens aufsitzen und gehen könntest?"* (Therese, would it not cause joy to you if you received some relief of your suffering, at least to be able to sit up and walk again?) Therese answered, *"Mich freut alles, was vom lieben Gott kommt."* (Anything that comes from God causes joy in me.) Again the voice said: *"Resl, eine kleine Freude will ich dir machen, du sollst aufsitzen und gehen können, aber du wirst noch viel zu leiden haben; doch fürchte dich nicht; ich habe bisher geholfen und werde dir auch in Zukunft helfen."* (Therese, I shall give you a small joy. You shall now be able to sit up and to walk, but you will still have much to suffer. However, be not afraid; you have received help through me in the past and I will also help you in the future.)

As the saint spoke, it was as though two strong hands lifted Therese from her bed—and after being paralyzed for six and one half years, she found herself completely healed. Not only was she healed of the paralysis, but of the gaping sores on her body as well. According to medical reports, some of those sores were deep enough to expose bones. In a matter of seconds, the sores were completely healed and were covered with a fresh layer of skin.

On November 7, 1925, Therese again became very ill. She had a high fever and suffered terrific pain in the abdomen, and was unable to sit up in bed. The situation became so bad that on the 13th the doctor was rushed to her bedside. He diagnosed the illness as an acute attack of appendicitis and ordered her removal to the hospital at once. Arrangements were made for the operating room, and the time for the operation was set. According to the doctor, any postponement of his orders would result in serious consequences, and he could not take responsibility.

Father Naber was called to the house. Therese's parents thought he might persuade the doctor not to be too hasty, but the pastor told the Neumanns that they should consider the doctor's words as the will of God. Therese must be operated on, or she might die. Her father quickly prepared to get the cart ready, and her mother got busy preparing the necessary clothes and bedding. Therese herself told the doctor,

"If God wants it, I would let you cut off even my head."

Suddenly, Therese had a severe attack of pain, causing her to roll up like a ball, twisting and turning. Then, all of a sudden, she sat up in bed and watched something towards the ceiling with extreme eagerness. They heard her say "Yes" several times. After another attack of pain, she got out of bed and told her surprised family to help her get ready to go over to the church and say the "Thanksgiving prayers" which St. Therese had ordered her to say. Therese Neumann had again been completely cured.

— Chapter 2 —

THERESE RECEIVES
THE WOUNDS OF CHRIST

As morning approached on the first Friday of Lent, March 5, 1926, Therese had a weak spell which forced her to stay in bed. She was alone in her bedroom during most of these hours, in a condition which seemed to be a state of semi-consciousness. Sometime before noon Therese returned to normal. She made no comment as to what had happened to her during those hours.

While recuperating from this condition, she noticed in surprise that her nightgown was stained with blood on her left side. She found that the blood came from a wound slightly above her heart. Not wanting to cause her parents any further anxiety, she decided not to tell anyone about the wound, feeling certain that it would soon be healed. Therese managed to clean her side satisfactorily, and she hid the cloth under the mattress of her bed. The wound, about one and one half inches above the heart, was the first of her stigmata and represents the place where the lance of Longinus penetrated the sacred body of Jesus. The wound was about one and three-eighths inches in length and three-sixteenths of an inch wide.

The week following the appearance of the wound brought no change in the ordinary routine of Therese's everyday life, until the next Friday approached—March 12, the second Friday of Lent. On Thursday night Therese suffered repeated attacks of weakness, which again forced her to remain in bed on Friday. This condition was followed by an ecstatic vision in the morning hours of Friday. Much to Therese's surprise, the heart wound bled for the second time—a fact which she treated in a rather superficial manner, not knowing the full significance of all these occurrences. It was about this time that she confided in her sister Creszentia, telling her about the wound above her heart. On this Friday no additional wounds appeared.

The third Friday of Lent, March 19, brought a repetition of the weak spells, and the wound on her side bled for the third time. This alarmed Therese and her sister—for in their childlike simplicity, they had thought the wound would surely heal.

As the fourth Friday, March 26, approached, the same affliction came upon Therese, and it was followed by a vision in the morning. During the ecstasy Therese received the outer wounds on her left hand. No longer could this be kept a secret—nor could the wound she bore above her heart. Even the bloodstained cloths which Therese had tucked under the mattress were discovered.

Anxiety over Therese's health alarmed her parents, brothers and sisters. It is hard to imagine how stunned they must have been when they saw not only the wounds, but learned that Therese had experienced visions of Jesus the past three Fridays. On the first Friday of Lent, she had seen Jesus with three of His Apostles on Mt. Olivet; on the second Friday, the same vision came to her, and in addition, she saw the scourging at the pillar and the crowning of thorns. On the fourth Friday Therese's vision of the Saviour was extended to His suffering while carrying the Cross, and His first fall.

The complete Passion of Our Lord, from the Garden of Mt. Olivet up to His death on the Cross, came to Therese in an ecstatic vision which commenced about midnight on Holy Thursday in 1926, and ended with our Saviour's death on the Cross at three o'clock on Good Friday afternoon. The suffering which came upon Therese during those hours was so excruciating that words cannot describe it. From the additional wounds on her hands and feet, which were now all completely penetrating, blood flowed profusely, as it did from her eyes, rolling down both cheeks and collecting about her throat and chest.

The sight of the sufferer lying on her bed in this pitiable condition was almost more than her loved ones could stand. As the hours passed and her suffering increased, they realized that they were witnessing something of divine origin. Father Naber had intended to anoint Therese, giving her the Last Rites of the Church, but at three o'clock in the afternoon the ever-increasing, excruciating pain climaxed in the final death struggle. Then, abruptly, it ended, and Therese fell lifelessly back into her pillows, exhausted even beyond the last ounce of her strength.

After about an hour had passed, Therese gradually returned to her normal physical condition. Neither Therese nor anyone else knew of the penetrating wounds on her hands and feet until she had been washed and dressed in fresh clothing. Upon examination, it appeared as if the skin on her hands, feet and above the heart had been cut with a sharp knife. Therese felt constant pain in those areas.

During the morning hours of Easter Sunday, 1926, Therese had another ecstatic vision in which she saw the risen Christ, dressed in a white garment.

On many subsequent Fridays came a repetition of the suffering of the Passion of Our Lord. An especially noteworthy participation in the terrible drama came on Friday, November 5, 1926, when Therese received nine wounds about her head from the Crowning of Thorns, and also wounds on her shoulders and back. Thus the stigmata on the body of Therese Neumann became complete, including the wound above her heart, penetrating wounds on her hands and feet, the nine wounds on her head, and the wounds on her shoulders and back. Not one of the wounds ever disappeared; they never healed, and they were still imprinted on her body at the time of her death.

The wounds were brownish-red in color, covered by a fresh scab, slightly raised from the rest of the skin. I have touched the hand wounds on many occasions, and I can say honestly that the slightest scratch would have made them bleed, to all appearances. When she first received the wounds, doctors treated them with the best-known medicines and salves in an effort to heal them. The result was catastrophic. Blood and pus started to ooze through the bandages, so to prevent blood poisoning the doctors urged their removal.

Over and over again I am asked how many wounds Therese Neumann carried on her body as a stigmatist. My private estimate is in the neighborhood of 45: wounds on the feet— two; wounds on the hands—two; heart wound—one; shoulder wounds and wounds from the Carrying of the Cross— about 30. Then, too, Therese had nine distinct head wounds from the Crowning of Thorns. All together one can easily come up with the number of 45 plus.

The stigmata on Therese's hands were a constant source of suffering and annoyance in performing manual tasks, and the wounds on her feet made walking very painful. Therese's shoes were especially made to relieve the pressure on her wounds. They were fashioned with one strap near the ankle, so that her instep wound was free from pressure. She wore gloves when working, as the wounds on her hands were very sensitive. The palms of her hands were often protected by adhesive tape to keep the wounds clean and to protect the skin from being torn even more.

But despite constant pain, she was never idle for a moment. Besides performing the many tasks that absorbed her time and energy, Therese daily spent many hours in prayer. Thus she entered into what was to become a lifelong participation in the sufferings of the Saviour.

— *Chapter 3* —

THERESE'S SUFFERING
OF THE PASSION OF OUR LORD

I have spent many hours discussing the Passion with Therese and Father Naber. The Passion itself and the particular circumstances are well-known to us. Therese Neumann experienced ecstasies accompanied by the suffering of the Passion on the Fridays of Lent and Advent, and on a sufficient additional number of Fridays during sorrowful octaves to raise the total of this type of ecstasy to twenty-six, twenty-seven, or twenty-eight for the year—not all Fridays, as is sometimes assumed. (An octave is the eight-day period consisting of the seven days following a holy day, or "feast day," plus the feast day itself.) This means that approximately half of the fifty-two Fridays in the year were free from the suffering of the Passion. In 36 years she experienced Passion ecstasies some 725 times. These sufferings took place in exact conformity with the liturgical calendar of the Catholic Church. On Fridays during a joyous octave, or Fridays falling on a feastday of a particular saint, there were no Passion ecstasies; instead, Therese saw the saint's death or martyrdom (as the case might be).

During an ecstasy she was completely blind and dead to anything around her. According to medical experts, one could cut her with knives and stick her with needles and she would feel nothing. Her body was in Konnersreuth, but her mind and heart were either in Jerusalem, or wherever the many hundreds of visions originated. There was only one thing that brought Therese back momentarily, and it is very significant. If a Catholic priest was present at an ecstasy and gave Therese his blessing, she always reciprocated with

11

"Vergelts Gott, Pfarrer" (Thanks be to God, Father), or in the case of a Bishop, she would answer, *"Vergelts Gott, Oberpfarrer"* (Thanks be to God, Your Excellency). Many such instances are recorded, and I myself have witnessed it.

On ordinary Fridays the suffering started in the morning at about eight o'clock and lasted until three o'clock in the afternoon, when Therese died with Our Lord. At about five or six o'clock she was usually back to normal life. The Good Friday suffering started on the evening of Holy Thursday, when she fell into ecstasy and remained thus until the early morning hours of Holy Saturday. During the Passion she witnessed Our Lord in the Garden of Gethsemane, then Christ before the High Priests, the scourging, the crowning with thorns, the carrying of the Cross, Simon of Cyrene, Veronica, the Crucifixion, and Christ's death on the Cross. She found herself among the Apostles and she followed Our Lord closely, experiencing with Him all His agony and suffering, and even His death on the Cross.

According to Father Naber, Therese was told by Our Lord that she suffered the same physical and mental agonies as He Himself did for us. She also suffered the loneliness of the Cross. The ecstasy came to her in about forty-five scenes, which meant that after suffering four or five minutes, she fell back onto her pillows and had a rest period for a short while.

While I mentioned earlier that Therese died with Our Lord, that is exactly what happened. According to Father Naber, as well as pronouncements by medical doctors, she died with Jesus at three o'clock. Upon many careful examinations, it was found that she had no heartbeat, no pulse, and no breathing! She lay motionless, slumped against the pillows, for about forty-five minutes. Under normal circumstances, she would have been pronounced dead! Then, after about 45 minutes of being DEAD, she gradually came to herself and acted like a small baby, yawning and stretching. After an hour or so, she was right back to her normal life.

The amount of blood lost during the Passion ecstasies varied in the different sufferings. Those that took place during Lent were by far her greatest sufferings of the year. The Good Friday suffering was the longest and most severe. During this ecstasy, she lost at least one and one-half quarts of blood! All her wounds bled, while on other Fridays only the wounds on her hands, feet, heart, and head bled; her eyes also bled.

The way the blood flowed from the wounds defied the laws of nature. The mystic lay in bed on her back; her feet were at a normal ninety-degree angle, with the toes pointing toward the ceiling. When the first drops of blood appeared, corresponding to Our Lord's being nailed to the Cross, her feet bled—but the drops of blood did not run off the sides of the feet, nor over the ankles, as one might have expected. Instead, the blood moved upward, towards the toes, just as Christ's did as He hung on the Cross.

The same was true of the blood running from the hand wounds up toward the elbow. While experiencing a Friday Passion, Therese stretched her arms out, and at times the hands were much lower than the elbows. Still the blood kept flowing up, against the law of gravity. There are films in the archives to substantiate this fact.

While Therese cried normal tears as she watched Jesus being accused and mistreated, her tears turned into blood in a split second when Jesus was harmed in such a manner that His blood commenced to flow.

I have been present at several of her Friday ecstasies (including briefly, as a pilgrim, in 1928 and 1929). On October 13, 1950, my wife and I observed her suffering for about two hours, and saw with our own eyes the agony and gasping, and the constant flow of blood from her eyes, hands and head.

Such an ecstasy was described by my uncle, Msgr. Karl Vogl, in the *Katholische Kirchenzeitung* (*Catholic Digest*), Salzburg, Austria. He had been with Therese on the Thursday before and all day Friday, March 25, 1927. His brother, Msgr. Adalbert Vogl, was also present. Here is his description of Therese's ecstasy:

Towards twelve noon, my brother and I returned to her room for the third time. Behold again, what a pitiable sight before us! With collapsed cheeks, hardly recognizable, sitting in bed, a true, profoundly affected serious figure of sorrows. Her pale yellow face, encircled by bloody tears, her eyes pasted shut by her own blood which is streaming down both sides of her cheeks, onto her throat and chest. The bloody imprint of the wounds from the crowning of thorns is plainly visible like a wreath around her white headscarf. The linen jacket by the heart is also clearly soaked with her own blood, in spite of four thicknesses of cotton paddings. We notice also the flow of blood from each of the hand wounds crossing her wrists. They appear like red flowers on her pale, soft hands.

There she sits, struggling, shivering and crying since midnight for twelve long hours, in spiritual contemplation of the terrible suffering of the Son of God. Her mind is absent to everything around her; she hears, sees and knows nothing of this world. One feels convincingly that the curtain between the present and the horrible drama of Golgotha, 2,000 years ago, is lifted for her. The occurrence there is brought to her clearly, faithfully and alive, as a witness under the Cross. In compassionate love, she suffered the foreboding of death during the night, in the morning hours, the scourging and crowning with thorns, then the condemnation, the carrying of the Cross, the Crucifixion, and now the extreme mental expectation of Christ's death on the Cross. Affected to the innermost, there we stand, directly at the bed of her agony, continually beholding her blood-strewn and sorrowful face.

Having seen her weakness yesterday morning when, during Holy Communion, she had to brace her right arm with her left to make the Sign of the Cross; and for hours, now, she has been relentlessly struggling and suffering, both arms outstretched, with the most sorrowful gestures of arms and hands. Through these we were able to recognize and, for the most part, to follow whatever scene she was participating in. It is evident, we are now coming to the climax of the suffering. The end has been reached, the participation in the death of Our Saviour is at hand. What unusual grasping and interlocking of her arms, which she brings up to her face again and again with an unspeakable expression of pain! And yet, there is nothing about her behavior which is unworthy, fantastic or theatrical.

Thanks be to God, the agony of death has come to an end! Her body twinges and trembles all over. Jesus cries out His final *Consummatum Est!* to the world and then commends His spirit to His Father. Suddenly, the suffering body of Therese Neumann falls lifelessly back onto her pillows. The quietness of death governs the room. Is she truly dead? No breathing, not the slightest movement of the body discloses any sign of life. After a lapse of time Father Naber speaks to her. Life gradually reappears. She starts gasping for air; her throat is filled with mucous. Thirty minutes pass before she is finally relieved of this by vomiting. Again, she falls back onto her pillows, completely exhausted.

I must admit, I have not come here for the purpose of pious curiosity. The reason is far greater. During my many years as a priest, I have come in contact with many sick and hysterical persons in hospitals and elsewhere. My concentrated thoughts today, as I observed Therese Neumann's suffering, were directed to anything that I might hear and see which could give me a clue to solve these miraculous occurrences in a natural way. I admit, I am a completely conquered and beaten man!

Unusual as it may seem, Therese never seemed to dread the coming of any Passion suffering. She even looked forward to being with her Saviour to try to alleviate His suffering by suffering with Him. But her suffering was so great that Our Lord gave her a few minutes of rest every now and then. After the rest she remained, of course, in ecstasy in bed, just resting, until the time was up and she again fell into the most excruciating pain, continuing the Passion.

The room where Therese suffered the Passion was directly

above the living room and kitchen of the Neumann home. A narrow flight of stairs led to the room. Across the bedroom, against the wall that was opposite the door, there was a small altar between two windows, where the great Cardinal Faulhaber—that courageous Prince of the Church who confronted Hitler at every turn—frequently offered Mass. Along the wall on the left was Therese's bed and a glassed-in cabinet where mounted butterflies, sent to Therese by missioners in the tropics, presented a veritable kaleidoscope of color. All along the wall to the right of the door was a large built-in bird cage filled with canaries and other beautiful birds that were reminiscent of the special interest of the great St. Francis of Assisi. In the center of the room was a small desk, pretty well covered with correspondence.

Today this room is preserved as it was during Therese Neumann's life. With my wife and others I was able to see it twice, in 1983 and 1985.

— *Chapter 4* —

THERESE AND
THE HOLY EUCHARIST

From 1922 until her death in 1962, Therese Neumann took no earthly food; beginning in 1926 she took no water, either. The sole nourishment of her body was the Holy Eucharist, received daily.

Therese had been a daily communicant from her childhood, and except for the days when the nature of her suffering made it impossible, she never failed to receive the Holy Eucharist. The usual time for her Communion was during the seven o'clock Mass. She received the regular size Host.

Some years ago, on Holy Saturday, two priests came to visit Therese. It was about noon when they arrived at the parish house to visit with Father Naber before going to the Neumann home. At about two p.m., Father took the visitors to the Neumann home to introduce them. As they walked into the room, Therese was still in bed recovering from the ordeal she had been through on Good Friday. On that day she had suffered much for others, commencing where the Passion left off. She had, therefore, not been able to receive Communion that morning.

All of a sudden, her suffering became very severe. The movements of her body and the expression on her face left no doubt that she was in great pain. Mucous and blood were ejected from her mouth, and to the surprise of the priests present, the Sacred Host which she had received in Holy Communion on Holy Thursday appeared on her tongue.

I asked Father Naber several times to describe the appearance of the Host when this happened. He said that the Host was slightly damp and a little curved, but that otherwise It was the same as when the priest had given It to her in Holy Communion. This re-appearance of the Host occurred frequently and was recorded up to the 22nd hour after she had received It on ordinary days. That is the reason why many priests and others have referred to Therese Neumann as a "living tabernacle." I agree. Moreover, back in the 1920's, Cardinal Michael von Faulhaber of Munich, great leader of the German Bishop's Conference, gave a Lenten sermon in the Cathedral of St. Michael in which he stated before a packed church that "Therese Neumann is a living tabernacle."

During a visit to Konnersreuth in September of 1950, I asked Therese what would likely happen to her if she were to receive Holy Communion only once a week. *"Dann wär es mit mir bald aus,"* was her answer (That would mean the end of me—soon). Her absolute need of Holy Communion for physical sustenance was the reason why the hours shortly before she received Communion were her most agonizing ones. The last Host she had received was then digested— after about twenty-two hours—and she felt that her life was ebbing away. That may well be why Our Lord granted miraculous Holy Communion when she was unable to receive at the regular time.

Then, too, there were times when Therese was suffering so intensely during the morning hours that she was unable to receive the Holy Eucharist. If the suffering subsided during the day, she would ask Father Naber to give her Holy Communion—and he was always happy to do so. On one such occasion, a priest was visiting Therese and he asked Father Naber if he might give her Holy Communion. This was agreed, and they went to the church and made preparations. Therese took her accustomed place behind the altar where she received the Eucharist. As the priest moved toward Therese, holding a Host above the ciborium, he was surprised to find her in ecstasy, with another Host visible on her tongue. Father Naber, as well as the other prelates and priests, had either had similar experiences while administering Communion to Therese, or had come to share the common knowledge of this phenomenon.

I had heard reports that sometimes when Therese was about to receive Holy Communion, the Host left the priest's fingers and was carried through the air onto her tongue. Anxious to clear this up in my own mind, I asked Father Naber about it. His answer was that to his knowledge this had never happened, but that, as in the instance related above, the Host at times reached Therese's tongue without being placed there by a priest. When the priest approached Therese with the Host, she was ready to receive, with eyes closed and lips parted.

At Communion time she often had a vision in which she saw the Saviour in bodily presence. Clothed in white and smiling, He benignly moved toward her. Therese's arms were outstretched, and she was almost lifted from the chair as she reached toward the Lord. Entirely absorbed in the vision, she did not see the priest, the chalice, or the Host. Her lips remained open while the priest placed the Sacred Host on her tongue. Without any perceptible movement of swallowing, the Host immediately disappeared. I have spoken to a number of priests who have seen Therese in ecstasy at Communion time and have also marvelled at the disappearance of the Host as it rested on her motionless tongue.

Other instances of Therese's miraculous reception of Holy Communion involved Father Wutz. Therese spent many days during her life at the home of this professor in Eichstätt, Bavaria. There she felt more at home than in Konnersreuth because there she was secluded from the many visitors. In Eichstätt she suffered and prayed without outside interruption. Her sister Ottilie and Father Wutz took the best of care of her, she had access to the private chapel, and she attended Mass and received Holy Communion daily.

Father Wutz knew much about Therese's mystical requirements. He was a very holy priest and also a professor of Oriental languages and the customs of the Holy Land in ancient times. All that Therese needed for her spiritual comfort was readily at hand.

During many intensive sufferings which she took upon herself for the sins of others, Therese became so ill that her sister and Father Wutz thought many times that her end was near. For this reason, Father Wutz kept a consecrated Host in the chapel tabernacle, to give to Therese whenever such a serious need would arise. One day, Ottilie called the priest to come immediately because Therese had suffered so much all day and was gasping for air as if she were dying. Other friends in the Wutz house also thought that was the proper thing to do.

Suddenly, Therese slumped back in her easy chair. She became full of joy, to the amazement of the bystanders. She opened her mouth, and a Host appeared on her outstretched tongue, only to disappear without any movement of swallowing. In the meantime, Father Wutz arrived and opened up the tabernacle—only to find that the consecrated Host, which he knew had been there, was gone! The Saviour Himself had again given Therese the Bread of Life! Also, on very high feastdays Our Lord gave Therese the joy of receiving the sacred Host directly from Himself.

Another such beautiful instance occurred one day while Therese was in her home in Konnersreuth. It happened that her brother Ferdinand was visiting their sister Ottilie and Father Wutz in Eichstätt. Ferdinand was there overnight as a guest, and Father Wutz consecrated two Hosts during the Mass. One Host was for Ottilie and the other for Ferdinand. During the offering of the Mass, Father Wutz saw both Hosts in the ciborium. The Mass progressed and it came time for Holy Communion. As he walked over to Ottilie with the ciborium in his hand, Father Wutz noticed, to his great astonishment, that there was only one Host left. He broke that Host in half and gave one piece to Ottilie, and one to Ferdinand.

This was discussed with quite some anxiety at the breakfast table. No one had an answer as to what had happened to the other Host.

About an hour or so later they received a telephone call from Therese in Konnersreuth, and she told them that the

Saviour had been so kind to her that morning during a terrible suffering. She said that because Father Naber was somewhat detained in celebrating Mass at the usual hour of 7:30 a.m., Our Lord had placed her in bilocation at the Communion rail in Eichstätt and given her one of the Hosts from the ciborium of Father Wutz. Therese then told Ottilie, to everyone's amusement, that the flowers on the altar were beautiful, "but they sure need watering badly!" That was indeed the truth.

One time Therese was visiting in the parish house in Konnersreuth because Father Naber had a priest visitor. While a friendly discussion was going on between the two priests, the Saviour informed Therese that there were two strange men milling around outside the church, cursing and using very foul language in relation to the life of Therese. Therefore, she assumed a very painful suffering during which she suddenly made a motion to be helped over to the church to receive Our Lord immediately. All three went over to the church, but before the priests had a chance to open up the tabernacle, Our Lord had already given Therese Holy Communion as she sat in her favorite place in the church. Both priests were witness to that.

During the five decades that Father Naber was the pastor in Konnersreuth, it would sometimes happen that he was on a sick call at the time for morning Mass. But from the 24th hour since her previous Communion, and even sooner, Therese would be on the verge of starving to death with an extreme longing for the body of her dear Lord. Father Naber being late for Mass, Therese would receive Holy Communion directly from the Saviour; He would take one of the consecrated Hosts from the tabernacle and give It to Therese. After Father Naber caught on to this system of Our Lord, he intentionally put one consecrated Host next to the ciborium in the tabernacle just for Therese, and that is the Host that disappeared on such occasions. Readers can believe this or not, but it is TRUE.

Therese had a special place where she sat in church. She

had so many wounds, hurting her to various degrees—diminishing in the presence of a priest or tabernacle, but always hurting. And it can be cold in Konnersreuth. Since she was spending so much time before the Blessed Sacrament, good friends made her a sort of stool, which looked like a confessional, and wired it up with a light heat pad. After being bothered and harassed by the faithful, who sometimes even cut off pieces of her garment, Therese was ordered by her pastor to place herself in that special chair behind the altar. (I sat in it, as did my fellow travellers, in 1983 and 1985.)

As explained in Chapter 16, any priest who gave Holy Communion to Therese on the Thursday before a Friday Passion ecstasy heard the voices of angels, one giving the other instructions to tell the priest that Therese should receive Holy Communion one hour earlier on Friday, the next day. In this way Therese would be able to receive the Bread of Life while she was still physically able to do so, before becoming enveloped in ecstasy. According to Father Naber, any priest present during Holy Communion on Thursday before a suffering would plainly hear the instructions of the angels.

— Chapter 5 —

ABSTINENCE FROM FOOD AND DRINK

In the years when she was suffering for the seminarian, Therese was not able to swallow the whole Host at daily Communion. Father Naber therefore decided that she should be given a very small particle of the Host and just enough water to enable her to swallow the sacred species. At this time, in the spring of 1922, Therese had lost the urge to eat anything whatever and felt no need for food. It is an established fact that after that time she did not take any solid food in any way, shape or form for the rest of her life; thus her total abstinence lasted 40 years. The infinitesimal amount of water which she used in properly swallowing the Host was not enough to sustain life. Even that bit of water was dispensed with in 1926, as we shall see.

Shortly before Christmas, 1926, Father Naber was away from the parish for a few days. A priest from a neighboring village said the Masses in Konnersreuth each morning and attended to the religious affairs of the parish. The short sojourn of this visiting priest—who, apparently inadvertently, omitted the sip of water that Therese had been given— introduced an important transition in the life of Therese Neumann. On his return to Konnersreuth, Father Naber—whether by divine inspiration or from his realization that the sip of water was utterly negligible as sustenance—did not require Therese to take any water from then on, either on the occasion of her Communion or at any other time. She subsisted and was nourished by nothing except the Holy Eucharist.

Therese Neumann is the outstanding example in modern

times of the miracle of inedia (the phenomenon of being able to go without food). As a matter of fact, nothing whatever, no matter whether it was in solid or liquid form, would remain in Therese's body. Even a drop of water that may have trickled down her throat in the process of brushing her teeth was immediately ejected. For this reason, she was unable to take any medicines to relieve her sufferings. Therese had no urge to eat anything, except Our Lord in daily Holy Communion.

Remarkable as this phenomenon was, it is by no means unprecedented in ecclesiastical history. Those who would presume to deny it in Therese's case because of its alleged impossibility would also have to deny all the other certified, incontestable cases of inedia that are found in the lives of other saintly and specially favored people.

The book entitled *Catholic Mystical Life* states that this phenomenon has only happened to saintly Catholic men and women who have been singled out to live in such a supernatural manner. The Patron Saint of Switzerland, St. Nicholas of Flüe, lived without food and water for over twenty years. His only nourishment was the monthly reception of the Sacred Host in Holy Communion. The stigmatic Augustinian nun, Ven. Anne Catherine Emmerich, lived for the twelve years prior to her death consuming nothing but daily Holy Communion and a daily glass of fresh well water.

Several additional examples of such cases include: Blessed Angela of Foligno, who lived thus for close to eight years; Elizabeth von Reute, for more than fifteen years; St. Lidwina of Schiedam, for twenty years; Dominika Lazzari and Louise Lateau, each fourteen years. All these cases were subjected to the most gruelling investigations from both sides, pro and con, and found to be authentic.

In not one of these cases has this supernatural phenomenon ever been "explained" by human investigations and laboratory tests. Such unusual occurrences are an act of God, and man will never be able to come up with a valid explanation. I am one who believes that; I always have, and I always will.

"One very important reason which leads us to believe in the unquestionable genuineness of Therese's total abstinence from food is the fact that Therese is deeply grounded in a peculiar phenomenal relationship with the main ecclesiastical Sacrament, namely, the Holy Eucharist or the Last Supper." So wrote a priest who was present on the eve of a Palm Sunday.

An assistant priest once asked Therese the question, "Don't you feel any hunger?" She answered immediately, "You know that I don't eat!" The priest continued, "Do you want to be greater than the Saviour? While on earth He ate like we do." Therese laughed out loud and answered unswervingly, "The Saviour is able to do everything. Or don't you know that He is almighty?" Then she turned to the priest once more and continued with great emphasis: "Father, the result from nothing remains nothing. I do not live on nothing. I live on our Saviour. He revealed to us: 'My Body is truly a food.' Why should this not truly be the case, if it is His will?"

Despite the fact that Therese ate no food except Holy Communion from the spring of 1922, she steadily gained weight. When she was investigated in July of 1927, Therese weighed 121 pounds. In 1935 she weighed 140 pounds. During my visit with her in 1945 she weighed in excess of 185 pounds; in 1950 she weighed over 200 pounds, and in 1953 her weight had reached over 215 pounds!

I mentioned to Therese in 1953 that she had gained weight since I last saw her. Her laughing reply was, "I will no doubt be as heavy as my grandmother!" She, too, was a large woman and weighed in the neighborhood of 260 pounds.

In 1945 I had jokingly asked her what she had done with her ration cards during the war. She laughed and replied, "You know, Mr. Vogl, there are many mouths to feed in the Neumann family!" (Actually, she gave them to the poor, as she herself told me on another occasion.)

It is considered noteworthy that Therese's teeth, too, did not suffer from her abstinence from food and drink. Her teeth were as normal as anybody else's—and maybe better.

— *Chapter 6* —

THERESE DID NOT SLEEP

Another phenomenon which has occurred in the lives of many mystics is that of requiring very little rest or sleep. This was characteristic of Therese Neumann, too; she required little or no sleep. She was known to relax for about thirty minutes on some days, but not every day. Her resting consisted of meditation and other spiritual relaxation. From about 1926 on, normal human sleep was a thing unknown to her. Father Naber told me this several times.

Despite the fact that she did not sleep, Therese had wonderful energy. After being with her for many days, we were half dead in the evenings, yet she was as chipper as a little boy or girl full of energy and vitality.

If anyone saw Therese walk home in the middle of the night from the nearby church, he should not have been surprised. One of her favorite chores was to arrange the flowers on altars and elsewhere in the church, and to keep the house of God immaculate. She loved to do this work in the quiet hours of the night, and it was often way after midnight before she returned to her home. The good people of Konnersreuth knew that it was her ordinary routine to be at the church at night.

— *Chapter 7* —

THERESE NEUMANN'S VISIONS

Whole volumes of books could be written if one were able to record all of Therese Neumann's visions. For this, one would almost have to see the official archives, which are in Konnersreuth and Eichstätt.

Besides often seeing and visiting with Christ in her daily Holy Communion, Therese also saw Him on numerous occasions during the day when He appeared to her for various reasons. Then, daily, she saw the death of saints—either one or more on any day, corresponding to the liturgical calendar of the Roman Catholic Church. She knew that calendar better than many clerics did. (I was present at a vision of the death of St. Teresa of Avila and at a vision of the death of St. Lawrence, who was martyred by being roasted to death on a gridiron; after the latter vision Therese was so exhausted that she could hardly speak to me.) That makes 365 visions with just one each day, but many times she had three or more visions on the same day. My wife sat in the back seat next to Therese during our car trip in September of 1950, and she told me that during each hour Therese was in ecstasy for minutes at a time—and then she would suddenly be back to normal life, continuing the conversation that she had started earlier.

Therese sometimes bilocated to see people in other places, including the United States, India and other countries. Father Naber told me personally on various occasions that Therese experienced the sufferings of Christ from 26 to 28 times each year—on the sorrowful Fridays of the Catholic year. It has been estimated that she suffered the Passion not less than 725 times starting in 1926 and ending in 1962. Then too, at night while cleaning the parish church (she required no human sleep), Therese had visions all the time—she told me so. She often talked to and visited with the suffering Christ hanging on the cross in St. Lawrence Church in Konnersreuth. (This crucifix is still there.)

We know from personal observation that while having a vision of the death of a particular saint, Therese participated in the life of the saint with all her normal senses. She felt the cold or the heat, whichever the case might be; she saw the surrounding area and talked about the different architecture, for instance; she felt the pain and the joy, and she smelled the flowers and fragrances that the saints experienced. Experts call this "mystical sensitivity."

Therese told us that visions of many saints, as well as her visions of Our Lord Himself, were so beautiful in color and lights, and were so bright, that the sun in normal life appeared to her as being dark and somewhat dead by comparison. The Saviour always appeared to her in the brightest and most brilliant light. She told us that Christ, the Blessed Virgin Mary and Elias appeared in a corresponding light as forms made of "flesh."

On All Saints Day Therese experienced a 24-hour-long ecstasy in which she would see and visit with various saints from Heaven. On the following day, All Souls Day, she would have a 24-hour-long ecstasy in which she would see souls from Purgatory. On these two feastdays Therese saw all her visitors at the age of 33. This is in line with the theory of St. Thomas Aquinas. On All Souls Day she saw the recognizable forms of the dead in various shades of light, from fairly bright to almost dark.

Many times during the year Therese had visits from angels, high and low, particularly guardian angels. However, as she put it very plainly, she recognized them, as they appeared in bright light, but they were of an indistinct stature.

One time Therese reported to a very enthusiastic group of priests and people regarding her latest vision of St. Mary Magdalen, and of how she had poured a highly fragranced liquid type of spice over the body of the Saviour. She also saw the saint rub a textured salve on the feet of the Master. Therese smelled these fragrances, and explained after the ecstasy what she had experienced.

The visions were always the exact drama of the daily Gospels and writings in the Bible, or they were true excerpts of teachings of faith according to the various feastdays. The Saviour frequently let Therese know that the reason she was favored to visit with some of the early saints was that they had been with Him while He was on earth. In this class, of course, are the Apostles, the Blessed Virgin, Mary Magdalen and Martha, to name but a few. Therese also enjoyed ecstatic visions of other later saints, particularly because they were so revered by her as a child and also in her adult years.

Aside from her visions of the Passion of the Saviour, the visions which Therese is known to have experienced are manifold. As I glance at some of my notes from Konnersreuth, I shall list only a few:

The birth of Christ in Bethlehem.

The murder of the Holy Innocents by Herod (55 in Bethlehem, 19 in surrounding territory.)

Jesus, 12 years old, teaching in the Temple.

Jesus with the Samaritan woman near Sichem.

Jesus brings a dead youth back to life near Naim.

Presentation of the Child Jesus in the Temple.

Jesus healing a deaf-mute boy, who was also possessed.

Jesus driving the money-changers from the Temple.

Jesus being tempted by the devil.

Jesus praying on Mt. Olivet (Feast of the Precious Blood— Therese's heart wound bleeds).

Jesus preaching from the boat of St. Peter.

Jesus multiplying the fishes.

Jesus appears to the Apostles on Mt. Thabor.

Jesus visits with seven Apostles on Lake Tiberias, and appoints St. Peter to guide His Church, and foretells His death on the Cross.

Jesus appears to St. Thomas and the other Apostles after

the Ascension.

The death of the Blessed Virgin.

The Assumption of the Blessed Virgin.

The flight into Egypt.

The journey of Mary and Joseph to Bethlehem before the Nativity (Therese walked right beside the animal and St. Joseph).

The journey of the Kings to Bethlehem.

Frequent visions of St. Therese of Lisieux (The Little Flower).

Death of St. Teresa of Avila.

The finding of the True Cross by St. Helena.

The death of St. Aloysius.

The martyrdom of St. Lawrence.

St. Peter and St. Paul in prison.

The martyrdom (crucifixion upside down) of St. Peter.

The appearance of the Christ Child to St. Anthony of Padua.

The eating of the Paschal lamb in the home of Lazarus in Bethany.

The stigmatization of St. Francis of Assisi.

The death of St. Wolfgang.

The martyrdom of St. Cecilia, St. Catherine and St. Barbara.

The death of St. Francis de Sales.

Therese would see these visions over and over again. I do not know how many such visions are recorded, but I am sure they would run into the thousands. Therese also had other ecstasies in which the saints, souls in Purgatory, and members of the Church Militant living in other regions— such as the Holy Father—were present to her preternatural gaze. Many of her ecstasies came upon her with little or no warning, and sometimes she had no chance to adjust herself to the transition. Suddenly transported into ecstasy, she once dropped a child she was holding; or, with less unpleasant consequences, she is known to have let a garden tool fall from her hands, or to have released some other instrument or article from her grasp. Sometimes ecstasies occurred in the midst of a coughing spell, or a flurry of laughter—and when the ecstasy had passed, the coughing or laughter would be resumed to its normal conclusion. The ecstasy kept her "frozen" in the position she was in when the ecstasy occurred, whether she had been sitting or kneeling or whatever posture she may have been in. As the ecstasy passed, she collapsed inert to the floor, ground, or into someone's arms.

One year on the feastday of St. Francis of Assisi, Therese was in ecstasy and lying on her bed with visitors around her. Suddenly she raised herself up; she was seeing the Saviour as He was just imprinting His wound marks onto the body of St. Francis. She recognized the mountain where this occurred as Mt. Alverna. After the vision and an "exalted rest" period she told the bystanders that she had also seen a cherub, a beautifully illuminated young man with very large wings, above whom the Saviour stood, in much greater illumination. While this was going on, she saw St. Francis kneeling reverently before Our Lord.

Therese made a remark, after this beautiful vision, that she was not worthy to carry the wound marks of Our Lord. She also felt herself not worthy to belong to the Third Order of St. Francis. A long fourteen years elapsed before she finally joined the Third Order conducted by Father Stanislaus, O.F.M. Cap., the Provincial of the Capuchins in Munich. As her heavenly sponsor on this occasion, Therese chose St. Clare of Assisi. Ottilie and Father Naber also joined the Third Order at the same time.

An incident which took place in 1940 included both vision and prophecy. Freiherr von Aretin, a German nobleman, scholar and writer and a good friend of Therese, wrote to her in June, asking for an appointment to visit her in July. She wrote back, telling him that he should not come to Konnersreuth before August 15th. He could not understand the delay. A week or so after Therese received his letter, she, Father Naber and a doctor drove to Eichstätt to attend the first Holy Mass of a priest who had become a convert in Konnersreuth, and on the way home, Therese had a stroke that paralyzed her right side. Although she was given expert medical care, her condition remained very serious.

Then on the Feast of the Assumption, August 15, Father had several visiting priests to help him with the special services. Knowing that the visitors would like to speak to Therese and that Therese would enjoy meeting them, he had her brought to the parish house, where she could lie on the couch in the living room. Dinner was about to be served. Everyone was present in the room, awaiting the blessing to be said before the meal.

At the first stroke of the Angelus at noon, Therese was observed to be in ecstasy. Her left hand was outstretched and her body was raised up from her pillows as she smiled and reached toward someone who was visible to her alone. Her expression was one of great joy and happiness. Because of her paralyzed condition, she was unable to move any part of her right side. Her right arm still hung helplessly on the couch.

Suddenly, Therese dropped back against the pillows and fell into the *"erhobene Ruhe,"* which is the time immediately after an ecstasy, referred to by Father Naber as "exalted rest." A few minutes after that she awakened—completely recovered from the paralysis. There was not a sign of any sickness whatsoever! She explained that she had seen the Blessed Virgin who, accompanied by two beautiful angels, came to her out of a bank of fleecy clouds and restored her to perfect health. Apparently Therese had foreseen her incapacitation and restoration back when she sent her reply to Freiherr von Aretin.

A person who received a personal account of one of Therese's visions was Dr. Fritz Gerlich, who stopped in Altötting during Christmastime of 1929 to visit my parents and my uncle, Msgr. Adalbert Vogl. Dr. Gerlich was on his way home to Munich from Konnersreuth. He was overjoyed because Therese had told him in detail of the vision she had had of the birth of Christ.

Dr. Gerlich described Therese's vision. It went like this: In bilocation Therese found herself outside Bethlehem, before a wooden barnlike structure which was built up against a stone hill, with a roof slanted toward a field. Therese stepped inside the front gate and remained there. Toward the back, inside the barn, she saw eight posts about three feet high fastened into the ground, and two of them toward her right, but also to the back. Between the posts in the back there were five cribs, and next to a post by the second crib was a donkey, tied to it. In the middle of the barn was a crib made of boards and fastened onto two crossbars. There was a window on the right side, close to the front entrance, and a fireplace between the window and the right corner from the entrance. To the left, in the corner, was a pile of reeds. The Christ Child was born there. Therese was told who it was, and the Child was placed on it after being wrapped in a blanket. From where Therese stood, by the front entrance, she saw that the Child was facing toward the back. The Blessed Mother was on the right of the crib as seen from the entrance, and St. Joseph was on the left. He prayed with his hands clasped together, and Mary did so with her hands crossed at her breast. The time was given as December 24, 11:13 p.m., according to Therese's vision.

Dr. Gerlich was overjoyed in telling my folks about the beautiful vision Therese had had of the birth of our Saviour. He gave my uncle a drawing of Christ's birthplace. On account of the house searches by the Gestapo, many documents were ransacked by the secret police. (Dr. Gerlich, as well as my Uncle Adalbert, was brutally executed by the Gestapo.) However, the drawing had amused my aunt so much that she somehow copied it and saved it. (See the illustration section of this book for a copy of this picture.)

During this glorious and joyful vision, Therese had just smiled and was full of happiness, which all the bystanders shared. After midnight Mass, Therese had another joyful vision. Again she found herself in front of a stable, about a one-half hour walk from Bethlehem. As she walked away from the town, it was 50 yards on the left side of the road. The meadow was very uneven, and the stable was about seven feet high, covered with reed and also built against a hill. This stable was only about half as big as the one in which Christ was born. Inside the stable Therese saw various types of blankets and furry garments. Eight shepherds were occupying the place, with thirteen sheep and several white and brown sheep, and two dogs—one black, the other one brown. Outside of the barn was a fenced-in area with several hundred sheep. It was dark and dreary.

Suddenly, to Therese's surprise, it became bright and everything was beautifully illuminated. The shepherds rushed out of their quarters and in amazement saw a brightly illuminated young man above the stable, at a height of about three yards. The young figure was dressed in a pure white garment with long, wide sleeves; the robe reached down to his ankles, and he wore a belt about his waist. His hair was parted in the middle, and his left hand was on his chest; the right hand was raised toward the sky. Not only was the stable brightly lit, but the whole surrounding area was also illuminated. To Therese's amazement, the angel did not have wings. The messenger spoke to the shepherds in their language (which, of course, Therese understood), and he pointed to the left several times.

Suddenly, this messenger from Heaven was surrounded by hundreds of angels (Therese told me 600). They were not only singing beautifully, but were accompanied by string and wind instruments. Again the angel spoke to the shepherds, and then he disappeared. After some deliberation, the shepherds, followed by thirteen sheep and two dogs, walked briskly toward Bethlehem. To their surprise, they saw a brilliant light shining from a stable which also belonged to their master. Their joy was immense when they saw the Christ Child with Mary and Joseph. This vision was separate from another one, which followed, in which Therese witnessed the celebration of the shepherds at the sight of the Christ Child.

In notes given to my uncle, Msgr. Adalbert Vogl, by Dr. Gerlich is a very interesting account of Therese's vision of the Holy Innocents who were slaughtered at King Herod's command. There were 74 infants—55 from Bethlehem and 19 from the surrounding area. After the ecstasy in which she saw the babies brutally murdered with a three-ft.-long sword through their chests and then thrown into a corner, Therese had a pause from this dreadful experience. She then saw the 74 souls, like beautifully illuminated angels, flying happily above the stable of Christ, high up in the sky, singing heavenly melodies while moving in a circle over the stable. Suddenly, they all turned in a southwesterly direction toward Egypt and also flew in circles for a while over the place where Mary, Joseph and the Christ Child were traveling on their way to Egypt after escaping from Bethlehem. Then suddenly they ceased and all flew skyward into the heavens. Therese also reported that these "angels" wore beautiful white garments which reached from the neck to the ankles.

During the thirty-six years of Therese's mystical and stigmatic life, we have firmly established, according to all the intellectuals and people who have talked to Therese, what she actually saw in the thousands of visions during this long period of time. With all of us she shared the beauty of those visions; some were joyful, while others were very sad. Of course, the highlight for Therese was when Our Lord appeared to her. With great joy in her heart, Therese explained as best she could that Christ always appeared to her in body glorified, while pure spirits, such as angels and souls of deceased persons, appeared in illuminated human forms. The *"Heiland"* ("Saviour") always appeared in the brightest imaginable brilliancy; the Blessed Virgin Mary and Elias were less bright, but in pure flesh, as was Christ.

Deceased faithful, particularly on All Souls' Day, visited with Therese, as she told me, as if her home were an "open house." These holy souls were in human forms, illuminated through and through in white light which ranged from pure white to dark gray. Therese told me that it took a number of years for her to have the proper discernment of all these wonderful manifestations. It was as if she started out from a grade to move up to a higher one as time went on. She always saw angels in an illuminated form like the Holy Souls, but they were in a very bright light.

A particularly beautiful day was the celebration of All Saints' Day, when the "open house" again lasted all day. Two days after such an occasion (1953), I visited Therese with a friend of mine, Brother Krispin, O.F.M. Cap., from Altötting. She told us very vividly that the Patriarchs, Apostles and Evangelists came first, early in the morning. She mentioned other groups, but this is an example of what she told us. The martyrs came long before the other saints. On that day she was so kind as to tell me, and to stress the fact, that my Uncle Adalbert came long before Uncle Karl, as Uncle Adalbert was with the martyrs' group. (Adalbert came at about 9 a.m. and Karl at about 3 p.m.) She described my Uncle Adalbert as a venerable, holy priest with nice bushy hair. He looked to her like a man of 33 years of age. When my uncle was executed by the Gestapo in 1945 he was all gray and the top of his head was bald. Uncle Karl had also been bald at his death, and he too appeared with a full head of hair, as Therese laughingly told us. She got a chuckle out of this.

Brother Krispin came up with the question: If the visitors are all at the age of 33, what about those people who had no legs, no arms, etc., etc., and those who were blind? With great emphasis Therese replied that "all are perfectly undefiled and fully mature."

The 17th of September is the Feast of the Stigmata of St. Francis of Assisi. On this day Therese watched, in a beautiful vision, the stigmatization of this great saint. She saw the transfigured body of Our Lord, in the brilliant heavenly illumination, as He placed the stigmata on the body of St. Francis. According to Therese, this happened on the mountain she called "Alvernoo." After the vision Father Naber asked her who the first stigmatic was after Our Lord ascended into Heaven. She did not hesitate one moment, and named "St. Paul." Fr. Wutz studied this case, along with other qualified scholars, but came to the conclusion that no one ever saw the stigmata on St. Paul. However, further study revealed that St. Paul himself wrote a letter addressed to the Galatians, in which he stated: "I carry the stigmata of the risen Saviour on my body."

On October 15, 1953, I returned to Konnersreuth to visit Therese again. This visit was especially memorable because it allowed me to witness Therese as she experienced one of her visions.

After Mass, I had a long visit with Father Naber, Therese and her sister. It happened to be Therese's namesday (the Feast of St. Teresa of Avila, Therese Neumann's patron saint), and she was in a rather festive mood. She rarely experienced any suffering on feastdays, unless the sufferings were closely associated with a saint who was a martyr.

During our conversation, Therese expressed a desire to do some shopping in Marktredwitz, a town about ten miles from Konnersreuth. She accepted my offer to drive her there. Her little niece went with us.

One of the stores we visited was a pet shop. Therese loved birds, and I thought for awhile that we would never leave. She could readily identify every species, and she named every species in the store. She was particularly interested in one bird. I had been hoping for such an opportunity, so I told her the bird would be my namesday gift to her. She was so happy about getting the bird! Then I told the salesman we must have the best feed for it. There, again, she showed her knowledge. The man had to mix the seed in just a certain way. I had been shopping with Therese several times before, and I say in all sincerity, that was an experience! When we were shopping in a religious goods store on another occasion it was apparent that Therese was an extraordinary customer. She would choose only articles and pictures that bore a close resemblance to Jesus, the Blessed Virgin and the saints as she saw them in her visions.

Towards noon we drove back to Konnersreuth. I was invited to have lunch at the parish house, where Therese was as much at home as in her own home. She was like any other gracious hostess. She set the table with quiet deftness and waited on Father Naber and his guests. She was very attentive in supplying everyone's needs and constantly asked if there was anything she could do for us. I have had breakfast, dinner and supper with them day after day. Therese, who never ate, was always a perfect hostess. During breakfast on one occasion, when my wife was present, I had the common difficulty of keeping the honey from dripping off my biscuit. Therese came over to me and said, "I will show you how to avoid that." She quickly mixed the honey and butter and applied the thickened honey to my biscuit. That solved my difficulty. My wife and Father Naber received the same solicitous service.

During dinner we made arrangements to drive to Tirschenreuth to visit a friend who was sick in the hospital there. Therese mentioned that Father Naber should first take a little rest, and I should return at about three o'clock. At that time the three of us drove to Tirschenreuth and visited the friend.

At about five o'clock we were ready to return to Konnersreuth. As I was driving home, Father sat with me in the front seat and Therese sat alone behind us. I shall never forget that day! We came out of a forest to a small incline on the road; to our right were wooded hills. I turned and asked Therese if the hills ahead of us were still in Bavaria, or if they were behind the Iron Curtain. Therese did not know, and tapped Father Naber on the shoulder to ask him. Just as he turned to answer, Therese was in ecstasy! The transformation occurred in an instant. I pulled over to the side of the road and stopped the car. Father Naber said, *"Die Resl sieht jetzt den Tod her Hl. Theresia von Avila."* (Therese is seeing the death of St. Teresa of Avila.).

Therese's arms were outstretched and she looked around, obviously intently watching things that were hidden from our view. Suddenly, she leaned forward in an attitude of amazement and joy, extending her arms until her fingertips were at least even with us in the front seat. Then she fell back into her original position and folded her hands and raised them to her face. She then remained in an attitude of sorrow for several minutes. Again, she lifted her head and stretched her arms outward and upward while she seemed to be gazing at something which must have been very beautiful.

When the vision was over, she settled back in the seat, with her hands resting in her lap. Father Naber explained the vision to me (Therese had had the same vision before), and he said that Therese was now in a "rest period" after the ecstasy. He said that during this time she was utterly exhausted, and judging from her appearance, that was obviously true. Occasionally she yawned, and she reminded me of a child waking up from a deep sleep.

The vision had begun at 5:21 p.m. and it ended at 5:40 p.m. The rest period took another twenty minutes. When Therese returned to normal, she looked at us in surprise and wanted to know why we were stopping. Then she said, *"Gelt, Herr Pfarrer, jetzt ist die heilige Theresia auch gestorben."* (It's too bad, Father, but now St. Teresa died too.) She complained about the cold, to which Father answered, "Yes, surely, you were in Spain where it is warm! We don't have weather like that here."

Father Naber told me some of the highlights of the vision. Teresa of Avila died in Alba de Tomes, Spain. Several sisters and friends were gathered around her makeshift bed. Our Lord appeared and laid His hands on her. When Teresa of Avila died, her soul seemed to take flight from her body in the form of a white bird. Therese Nuemann had seen all this exactly as it had happened. The spot where the vision took place, about a mile south of Mitterteich, will ever be a memorable one for me!

As the years went by and the mystic saw the visions over and over again during ten, twenty, thirty or more years, she reached deeper and deeper into their meaning and an understanding of what was taking place. Thus Father Naber once told a group of visitors, in his humorous way, that Therese was making progress. After the visions, one could tell how increasingly joyful Therese was as she went into every detail of what had happened.

*   *   *   *   *

Since this is probably the last opportunity for me to share my experiences with those who are willing to learn something about this great mystic, I have, at this time, decided to share several beautiful thoughts about Therese which are very dear to me.

As I have mentioned in another section, a most rewarding and informative trip began in 1975 when I had a great, unexplainable urge to fly to Bavaria. I contacted Dr. Sträter, S.J., the priest with whom I had become acquainted three years earlier when he took my first deposition regarding Therese Neumann. We became instant friends, each having a great trust in each other. So, here I was with this wonderful friend and priest. At that time he lived in Rottenburg, Bavaria.

Much time was consumed talking about the case of Therese Neumann. The discussions went far into the night. I was "in Heaven," simply for the reason that I could exchange views on a very high level.

Father Sträter then suddenly requested that, under these circumstances, I should by all means drive with him to Eichstätt to visit a woman named Anni Spiegl, a long-time personal friend of Therese, who could almost be classified as her personal secretary. His request was a command for me— and a delightful one, at that.

We arrived in Eichstätt and Father Sträter called Anni Spiegl; he was told that Anni would be most happy to see us, even though she was on her deathbed, dying of cancer. The visit would be highly desirable. We were shown into the sickroom and there she lay, looking as fresh and vibrant as a young teenage girl. There was no mention of pain—she was just happy to have us there. My introduction was the beginning of an instant and seemingly long friendship. All Father Sträter had to tell Anni was who I was, what I was doing for Therese, that I had written one book, that I gave lectures in the States, etc., etc. The date was September 12, 1975. Anni informed us that she had less than two months to live. She was almost in a state of "exhilaration." To be soon with Jesus and all the saints, to be with Therese and Father Naber and their friends—this was her desire, and she was waiting for the end. Anni died on October 24, 1975. She had predicted accurately.

During our visit and after she knew all about my activities, Anni got out of her bed and walked into another room. She came back with a book in her hand and gave it to me. She said: "Mr. Vogl, this is yours all the way through. Whatever you need from it to further your own desires regarding your writings—it's all yours."

I would be failing in my duties if I failed to mention Anni's sister. From the States I wrote to Anni to thank her for the great joy she had provided for the two of us. But it was too late. I received the sad news from her sister, Mrs. Maria Böhm, that Anni had indeed passed away in October of 1975. Since then I have corresponded with Maria every month. She is an informant for me of the highest magnitude. I now call her my "second mother."

Having said this I am now willing to share with my readers some of the material that Anni Spiegl gave me on her deathbed.

EYEWITNESS REPORT OF VISIONS EXPERIENCED BY THERESE IN THE PRESENCE OF ANNI SPIEGL
(Material given to me by Anni for my use.)

"Therese maintained intimate relations with the supernatural. I seldom heard her speak of God or Christ; for her there was the name 'Saviour.' Her whole being betrayed the intimate nature of her relationship with Him. Over the 36 years she saw, in her visions, the whole of His life on earth—His 33 years of public mission and the miracles He worked.

"She saw the land where Christ lived and worked, saw the people around Him, their houses and their customs. She heard their language. She went with Him from Bethlehem to His death on Calvary. She saw His Resurrection and His life continuing in the Church and His saints.

"I experienced Resl ['Resl' was Therese's nickname] during her visions. She did not wait for them to come or prepare herself for them. She was literally seized and suddenly torn away

in the middle of a conversation or work. I can still see her
before me with her knitting dangling in her hands during
a vision: she had not had time to put it down. When she
was in this state, one could touch her, or even put one's finger on her wide-open eyes, but she heard and felt nothing.
At such times she also stood with her soles flat on the floor
and only afterwards complained of the pain in the stigmata
on her feet. [As I have already mentioned, Resl usually walked
and stood on the sides of her feet since putting them down
flat put weight on the stigmata and caused her pain.]

"Resl was also present with all her senses in the land she
saw. You could see her shivering or feeling the heat, turning
up her nose at unpleasant smells or sniffing with relish the
aroma of herbs and ointments. Anyone who had the opportunity of watching Resl's facial expression during her visions
can no longer have any doubts as to their authenticity. Joy,
fear, amazement, inquisitiveness and horror passed over her
face in turn within a matter of seconds. Her face lit up with
a supernatural glow when she saw the Saviour or witnessed
a miracle, and she scarcely dared to breathe any more. I
shall now relate several visions which have remained in my
memory.

"According to Resl's description, the Blessed Virgin Mary
did not come from a poor background. She saw the house
of Mary's parents, Joachim and Anne, as a fine house of
stone such as only the wealthy possessed. Resl also saw Mary
at the Temple school in Jerusalem, and not all parents could
afford to send their children there. The poverty began with
the birth of the Child in the stable, but only because there
was no room at the inn; it went with them on their flight
into Egypt and from then on never left them.

"Resl saw Mary and Joseph on their journey from Nazareth
to Bethlehem. A she-ass carried their baggage, which Resl
described in detail, as she did the clothing of Mary and Joseph.
She saw them arriving exhausted in Bethlehem and looking
in vain for a place to stay. Immediately upon arrival they
went to register, although they had to wait for a long time

because of the crowds of people there. Resl then saw them
wandering out through the city gate to a stable, which she
described in detail. In a further vision she saw the Child
in the manger.

"At the Presentation of Jesus in the Temple, Simeon laid
the Child in Resl's arms, too. She was hardly able to bear
the bliss. It was the same when the two-year-old Child greeted
the wise men from the East. Resl, too, was allowed to give
the Child her hand, and she once fainted with joy at this.
She saw the visit of the Magi in several visions; she saw
each of them in their own country, and according to Resl's
description, all three were wealthy princes. Astronomy was
keenly pursued in their countries; they had their own as-
tronomers and built towers entered by rope ladders to observe the stars. When they saw the unusual star, they were
most astonished and sent messengers to each other. Then Resl
saw each of them setting off from his own country with a
large retinue, and she saw them meeting each other. Then
they followed the star together.

"The journey was long, and had to be made at night because the star was not visible by day. The Child Jesus was
already about two years old when they eventually arrived.
Resl described in detail the house over which the star stood
still; the star seemed to fall onto the house, and Resl saw
the animals rear up in terror. The Magi were disappointed
when they entered the house and saw the simple family with
the Child, but suddenly the divinity of the Child shone through
and they fell down and worshipped Him. Resl also saw all
the details of the massacre of the Holy Innocents in Bethlehem and then the flight into Egypt. The Christmas and Easter
periods were rich in visions, though throughout the year Resl
had numerous visions of the life of Jesus.

"[One time] we were in the Wutz house and had a large
number of visitors. Ottilie and I had made up beds for ourselves in the junk room and I had already gone to bed when
Resl came in late at night and said, 'I must just have a look
where you are sleeping.' I called to her, 'Put the light on

or you'll tread on me!' When she saw we had just mattresses on the floor, she laughed heartily. She sat down on a box and was telling me what had happened during the day, when suddenly she had a vision. It was on the Gospel of the day, the healing of the man born blind. At that time I was somewhat inhibited, and did not dare ask for details.

"Resl gave a very plastic description of the casting out of the devils from the possessed man in the country of the Gerasens. The devil asked the Saviour to be allowed to enter the herd of swine feeding nearby. As a country girl Resl understood the terror of the swineherds when they saw their herd rush headlong towards the sea, plunge in, and be lost for their owner. She recounted how heavily the beasts plumped into the sea, how the swineherds ran away, and how almost the whole town turned out and asked the Saviour to leave the area.

"Resl saw the raising to life of Jairus' daughter. She was horrified at the noise of the minstrels, and even more so at their laughing the Saviour to scorn when He said that the girl was not dead but sleeping. Resl described the house exactly, as also the bedroom and the girl herself. She was particularly delighted at the dismay of the minstrels when the girl arose.

"[On one occasion] Resl and I were visiting the Mother Superior and Sister Audita in the hospital in Eichstätt and were sitting together in animated conversation when, shortly before 11 p.m., Resl was suddenly snatched away. The sisters were frightened as they did not know what was the matter. Resl had a vision of the feeding of the five thousand, during which she showed herself to be a child of the country: how she lamented over the long grass being trodden down by the thousands when it would have made such good fodder!

"We were once visiting the cathedral priest, Rev. Kraus, who was parish priest in Buchdorf after his release from prison and expulsion from Eichstätt. We were already in the process of leaving and Resl was just saying good-bye to Father Kraus at the front door when she suddenly saw the Fall of the Angels.

It was the Feast of St. Michael. Afterwards she told us about it. There had been a mighty surging to and fro, for Lucifer was St. Michael's equal in might and size. The victory over Lucifer could be read on Resl's face and experienced with her.

"One Palm Sunday I had the privilege of being present at Mass in her room. During Lent Resl was unable to leave her room, and so it was a great concession on the part of the Bishop of Regensburg to allow Mass to be celebrated in her room once during Lent, namely on Palm Sunday. In her vision that day she saw the entry into Jerusalem and also the cleansing of the Temple. There was a look of satisfaction on her face when the buyers and sellers were driven out of the Temple and when the Saviour overthrew the tables of the money changers and the money rolled onto the ground. She was deeply affected when it came to the turn of the dove sellers; even during a vision her love of animals came out.

"Resl described the embalming and laying in the grave of Christ, down to the last detail. His whole body was swathed in linen cloths with bunches of herbs and essences. The head was wrapped in a cloth of its own. Resl wanted to help with the swathing, and made all the movements with her hands. After the Resurrection the linen cloths lay in the grave like an empty shell. The Holy Shroud of Turin may have been the linen cloth with which the Saviour was taken down from the Cross. That, too, was described by Resl.

"I also had the privilege of experiencing Easter at Konnersreuth. First of all, at five in the morning, I joined in the lovely custom of the women of Konnersreuth of visiting and venerating the crosses in the surrounding fields and the cemetery. After early Mass I was allowed to spend the whole day with Resl, who had several visions.

"She felt a special affection for St. Mary Magdalen, who must have been very beautiful. Resl encountered her in several visions. According to Resl she was the sister of Martha and Lazarus; she had her share of the inheritance paid out to her in cash and took up residence on her estate at Madgala, where she led a very frivolous life. She was beautifully dressed and ornamented; her ankles clinked softly as she walked. On her first meeting with Our Lord she merely wanted to see the good-looking, interesting man about whom the whole town was talking. With Mary Magdalen it was not a sudden conversion such as that of St. Paul. With her it was love, which first had to be chastened. She soon noticed that Jesus was different from the others, and sought to be near Him. Her conversion was complete when He said to her in Simon's house, 'Thy sins are forgiven thee, go hence in peace.' From now on she knew no more fear and there was no more going back.

"Thus Resl saw her spattered with blood beneath the Cross, and as the first to hurry to the grave on Easter morning; she was running, her lovely, full hair falling into her face so that she had to keep brushing it aside. Resl, too, made the appropriate movements with her. Mary [Magdalen] reached the grave first, while the other women remained standing some distance away. She found the grave empty and ran off to search the garden. Then she saw a man in front of her, whom she thought to be the gardener. She asked him, 'Where have you put Him?' Then came the reply, 'Mary.' At that moment Resl, too, recognized the Saviour and her face lit up with joy. (The first person Christ appeared to after His Resurrection was His Mother on Calvary.) In another vision Resl saw the Apostles hurrying to the grave. John got there first; however, he did not go into the tomb, but waited for Peter.

"On Easter Monday in her vision Resl accompanied the disciples on their way to Emmaus. You could tell that she was listening to their conversation. [You could see] the change in her expression when a stranger joined them and listened to them as if interested. With her hand she also made the gesture of urging the stranger to stay when he wanted to go on his way. Then came the sudden recognition of the Saviour when He broke bread. Afterwards she described how the disciples had run back without resting. It was also interesting that Resl had heard St. Peter preaching in German on Pentecost. Resl repeated what he had said and the gestures he had made; the miracle of the gift of tongues had taken place in her, too.

"On high feastdays or in connection with special events Resl already had visions before receiving Holy Communion. On such occasions she would not see the small white Host, but rather the Saviour Himself coming toward her. At such times the Host would enter her without her making any swallowing motions, and it happened that it was literally drawn out of the priest's hand. I was able to watch this clearly on two occasions.

"Shortly before Prof. [Father] Wutz's death it happened that in a vision of this kind the Saviour turned around and looked closely at the Professor, who was giving Resl Holy Communion. This frightened Resl. ('I know what it means when the Saviour looks closely at someone—He always wants something big.') Not long before, the Professor had returned from Dietzenbach, where he had sought a cure from a disease of the heart. Soon after Resl's vision he died of a heart attack.

"Resl saw not only Christ's life, Passion and death but also that of His Mother and the lives and deaths of numerous saints (one daily, and more)—all this in conjunction with the liturgical calendar of the Catholic Church. After the death of Jesus, Mary lived with John in Ephesus. She died, according to Resl's account, in Jerusalem. Resl saw the stoning of St. Stephen, and the work and death of the Apostles. She described in detail the martyrdom of St. Agnes and St. Catherine. She saw St. Francis at his stigmatization and death. In this way Resl saw and experienced the liturgical year of the Church. It often struck me that she continued to live only reluctantly, especially after beautiful visions. However, like everyone else she had a natural fear of death."

— *Chapter 8* —

THE LANGUAGE PHENOMENON

Another mystical gift possessed by Therese Neumann was the ability to understand foreign languages, especially Biblical languages. During the ecstasies of the Passion, she heard the four languages which were in common use during the time of Christ: Latin, Hebrew, Greek and Aramaic; the last-named was spoken in a dialect mixed with Greek words. Therese recognized and repeated them after she returned to normal life. The fact that this humble country girl could master such languages is a miracle in itself. Therese had a seventh grade education and did not speak or understand any other language but German; to her personal friends she spoke in the dialect of the Oberpfalz, the particular region of Bavaria in which Konnersreuth is located.

Many eminent scholars of Oriental languages and of the Old Testament have been available to Konnersreuth in order to check the authenticity of Therese's knowledge of languages. Nevertheless, it was indeed difficult to find scholars who were qualified to interview Therese. It is not an exaggeration to say that in many instances she knew more about these ancient languages and many other details than the scholars did!

Some of the noted men who helped extensively in the verification and clarification of the 2,000-year-old practices were: Rev. Prof. Dr. Wutz (a priest), professor of Oriental languages and the Old Testament at Catholic College, Eichstätt, Bavaria; Prof. Bauer, of Halle, a non-Catholic expert in Oriental languages; and Prof. Wessely, of Vienna, a non-Christian, who was also a scholar of these languages. The results of their investigations were made public.

These famous scholars came to the conclusion—and they

48

stated it categorically—that Therese's knowledge of these languages was absolutely correct, and that it was impossible for her knowledge to be explained by any falsehood or power of suggestion. Many other university professors who had similarly tested her came to the same conclusion. Dr. Prof. Wessely stated: "Therese Neumann's knowledge of Christ's own language is a miracle in itself. I am amazed at her knowledge of Aramaic in particular. It is *"Als etwas unerhörtes—noch nie dagewesenes."* (Something unheard of and inconceivable.)

My uncle, Msgr. Karl Vogl, knew Prof. Dr. Wutz very well and received a wealth of information from him. Every time he returned to his office in Altötting, I was right there to keep up with the developments on Konnersreuth. Through such reliable persons and many others of equal stature, as well as through my personal interviews later with Therese and Father Naber, I have been able to learn many interesting facts about her knowledge of languages.

During the vision when Jesus was near the city of Naim, raising a dead man back to life, He spoke first the word *"Etphetach,"* upon which the dead man opened his eyes and mouth. At the word *"Kum,"* he raised himself from the stretcher.

Therese pronounced certain words in connection with the Passion. Judas greeted the Master with these words: *"Schlama Rabbuni."* (Greetings, Master.) The other Apostles became aware of the fact that Judas would betray the Master, and cried out in excitement: *"Magera beisebua cannaba—magera beisebua."* (A sword, down with the man of the devil, that thief.)

The executioners inquired after *"Jeschua Nasarija"* (Jesus of Nazareth), and Jesus answered *"Ana"* (I). Then He turned to His Apostles and said *"Komu"* (Up). The people cried out, *"Ma hada?"* (What is the meaning of this?) Then later, Our Lord said, *"Amen, Amen amarna lachbam atte emmib pardessa."* (Amen, amen, I say to you, today thou shalt be with Me in Paradise.)

When Our Lord said, "It is consummated," Therese heard

in Aramaic, *"Schlem kalohi."* When He said the words, "Father, into Thy hands I commend My spirit," Therese heard *"Abba be ada afkid ruchi."*

The theory that Therese was able to read the minds of the various Oriental language scholars is disproven by the fact that she spoke the Aramaic sentences correctly to a degree which, at the time of her presentation to the experts, was not known to *them*. Furthermore, Therese used a constellation of Aramaic words, which no scholar expected, and yet she was entirely correct. In other words, Therese could not have read something from the minds of the learned men which did not exist in their minds.

In her visions of the saints, too, Therese was able to understand many different languages. The saints spoke in their native language, and yet Therese was able to understand them perfectly. There was never any language barrier with her. She always understood and repeated what was said, regardless of whether the saints were European, Asian, African or whatever.

Therese had hundreds of visions of saints during the year. On August 10, the Feast of St. Lawrence, St. Lawrence spoke to her in Latin. On the Feast of St. John the Evangelist, she heard St. John speak in Greek. When St. Therese of Lisieux appeared to her, she spoke in a French dialect that is used in the Pyrennees. St. Francis de Sales also spoke to her in French, while St. Anthony of Padua (who was born in Lisbon) spoke to her in Portuguese. St. Francis of Assisi spoke in Italian, and St. Teresa of Avila spoke Spanish. In the case of German saints, Therese would ordinarily understand it anyway, but the fact is that she then spoke a German accent that she normally did not speak—but she nevertheless repeated it perfectly.

As the years went by, the Saviour added a very special aspect to this gift by allowing Therese to hear the saints speak to her in her German dialect. This had also happened once on Pentecost Sunday, 1928, when she was bilocated to Rome and heard St. Peter giving a sermon in perfect German before the Coliseum. After one of these visions Therese reminded that Holy Scripture tells us that all those present on the first Pentecost, listening to St. Peter's sermon, heard it in their own native tongues!

— Chapter 9 —

MYSTICAL RECOGNITION OF PRIESTS, RELICS, THE HOLY EUCHARIST AND PRIESTLY BLESSINGS

It is common knowledge to many who visited Konnersreuth that Therese always recognized priests as priests. This was a particularly mysterious phenomenon which baffled many visitors.

One day a man dressed in the formal attire of a bishop came to Konnersreuth and visited Father Naber and Therese. Father Naber was very cordial to him, as he always was, but when Therese came into the room she immediately recognized that this was not a man with consecrated hands. She robustly put her hands on her hips and told him off in no uncertain terms, telling him to get out and stay out: "You imposter!" It was later reported to the parish that this man was arrested by the police as a con man who wanted to collect money under false pretenses.

Therese explained to me that she was able to recognize any ordained priest by his "consecrated hands." A priest might be working in a garden or wearing work clothes, but she would still know that he was a priest.

My wife and I learned firsthand during our trips with Therese and Father Naber that Therese also recognized the presence of the Blessed Sacrament in a church as far away as approximately one mile. When Father Naber asked her on several occasions, in locations unfamiliar to her, whether the Blessed Sacrament was present, her answer was always immediate and definite. When she approached the Blessed Sacrament—whether it was in the tabernacle of a Catholic Church or carried on the person of a priest making a sick call—her wounds reflected this joy, and the pain subsided temporarily.

Knowing that Therese always recognized a Catholic Church having the Blessed Sacrament present, a priest once asked her, "Is it also true that you can feel when a visitor has received Holy Communion?" "Yes," she said, "but only within a certain length of time."

Once while Therese was in ecstasy, a Benedictine priest came to the Neumann home in the company of other visitors. Shortly after they entered the room, Therese motioned to the priest to come nearer to her bed. Then she reached out and clasped a relic that was suspended from the Benedictine's habit. After holding the relic close to her heart, she kissed it. She explained that it was a relic of the True Cross, and further identified it as a particle from the lower section of the Cross, close to where the nail had transfixed the Saviour's feet. During the few moments taken to identify this relic, Therese's sufferings seemed to subside, but they resumed immediately thereafter.

On another occasion while Therese was in ecstasy, she asked a visiting priest to show her his rosary. When the priest handed it to her, she kissed it devoutly and explained that this rosary had once been used by Blessed Kreszentia of Kaufbeuren, Bavaria. The priest knew the history of this particular rosary to be precisely as Therese stated it.

On one occasion a gentleman brought a relic along from Italy. As Therese was touched by the same, she immediately responded that it was from a saint in Heaven who knew the Holy Father very well. She also told the name of the saint; it was Contardo Ferrini, who was not known at all in Germany and whose connection with the Holy Father was known by only a few trusted people. Again Therese startled the visitors by telling the incidents of his life, which they themselves did not know. It turned out that she was correct, as always.

We mentioned earlier that there was only one thing that would bring Therese out of a Passion ecstasy (momentarily), and that was the blessing of a Catholic priest or bishop who might be present. She would respond to the blessing with the words:

"Thanks be to God, Father," or "Thanks be to God, Your Excellency."

It happened one day while Therese was in ecstasy that a priest in the room blessed her secretly in his mind, and she acknowledged it immediately. However, the priest was so shaken by what he saw in that room, with blood running from her wounds, that he became overzealous and kept on blessing Therese. She finally motioned for him not to overdo it.

On Friday, October 13, 1950, my wife and I were present for the greater part of an hour during one of Therese's ecstasies. Other visitors on this occasion included Father Naber, two visiting priests, and the mother of one of these priests. One of the priests rested his hand on Therese's for a moment. As he did this, Therese asked, "What is this good man doing here? He does not belong here. I can't understand this."

Father Naber asked the priest whether he had ever walked along the Via Dolorosa in Jerusalem, the path that Christ had taken during His Passion. The priest replied, "Yes, I was there not long ago." This fact explained Therese's seemingly harsh question. She had recognized the visiting priest by his consecrated hands at the very time she was following Our Lord in ecstasy along the Via Dolorosa, where everyone else seemed to be an enemy of the Saviour. This had evoked the exclamation and gives further evidence both of the genuineness of Therese's perception of the temper of the Saviour's executioners and of her power to detect the identity of anyone consecrated to God.

The blessing of a priest was a very important part of Therese's life. Father Naber had a habit of blessing his parish, and Therese in particular, before he went to bed. On one occasion he had company, and he went to bed far after midnight. The next morning Therese told him in the sacristy, "Father, you surely stayed up late last night; I did not feel your blessing until [such and such a time]." Therese had told the pastor exactly when he went to bed.

Other priests also had the beautiful habit of blessing Therese, sometimes from far away. This was a great gift for the mystic because it always alleviated her constant suffering. When one of those priests came to Konnersreuth one day, Therese told him to the minute at what time he had gone to bed on the previous night. It all corresponded exactly to the way it had happened. Sometimes she also complained to priests who had forgotten to bless her at bedtime. Other times she cautioned priests to get more rest and go to bed earlier. Their blessing told her exactly what time they were retiring.

One day Therese's brother Ferdinand came home for a short visit. After greeting his parents, he entered Therese's room while she was in ecstasy. She drew him close to her, removed a newspaper from the inner pocket of his coat where it had been entirely concealed, and tore the paper into shreds. Ferdinand, as a civil service employee during the Hitler regime, was required to subscribe to the *Völkischer Beobachter,* a paper that was filled with Nazi propaganda and attacks on the Catholic Church. Ferdinand had specially secreted the paper on his person, and kept his overcoat on to further disguise its presence. His precautions, however, were unavailing, as Therese's ecstastic perception nullified all his efforts. When the ecstasy was over, Therese remembered nothing of the incident.

It is of additional interest that Therese tore the paper across its folds, which would normally have required many times the strength she possessed when not in ecstasy. A newspaper of similar size was folded like Ferdinand's and she was unable to make the slightest impression on it when she emerged from the ecstasy and was asked to attempt to tear it.

On another occasion during the Nazi regime, a layman entered Therese's room during the course of an ecstasy. Whether or not this man was a follower of Hitler, I do not know, but he was nevertheless carrying a picture of Der Führer in the inner pocket of his coat. When the man reached her bedside, although she was blinded by the blood that sealed her eyelids, Therese reached up, plucked the picture from the man's pocket, and tore it to bits, saying, *"Rauch und Feuer von der Hölle."* (Smoke and fire from Hell.) Thus did Therese's mysterious knowledge show itself once again.

— *Chapter 10* —

CURES, PROPHECY, BILOCATION, AND OTHER MYSTICAL GIFTS

Therese was instrumental in the cure of a man afflicted for years with multiple sclerosis. One day a lady from the Rhineland brought the man, her husband, to Therese. She rang the bell at Father Naber's rectory, having been told that Therese would be there. Therese was in meditation following a very hard day, and it had been planned that no one should see her for the rest of the day.

Father Naber went to the door, where he was greeted by the very concerned wife and her sick husband. Father was so shaken by the appearance of this man and, of course, the long distance they had travelled, that he influenced Therese to make another exception—which so often happened—and to see these people at least for a moment or so.

Therese spoke some very encouraging words, which she was able to do so effectively. She particularly stressed both the power of suffering and that of prayer in bringing us closer to Our Lord. Before she ended the visit, she turned to the wife and told her to cooperate with her and the husband and they would start a nine-day novena, the three of them, offering it up for the benefit of this sick man.

On the seventh day of the novena the man was healed instantaneously, while back in the Rhineland. Within a day or so, the pair again went to Konnersreuth to tell Therese and Father Naber what had happened. In thanksgiving, the family donated the majestic Swedish marble cross which now adorns the grave of Therese Neumann in the local cemetery.

It sometimes happened that Therese received mystical

knowledge of distant or future events. A medical expert had spent some time conducting a private investigation of the phenomena of Therese's experiences. He had concluded his observations and was leaving Konnersreuth in his car. Therese had a vision in which the Lord informed her that the doctor had made this investigation in order to publicize himself, and because of his pride and pretense of friendship, he was to be punished. A short time after his departure, word was received in Konnersreuth that he had had a bad accident. His car had careened off the road and struck a tree. The driver escaped serious injury, but the car was completely demolished.

On one occasion, in the 1930's, Therese's brother Ferdinand drove to Switzerland to show a film of a Friday ecstasy to some friends; the film was an excellent one. But Ferdinand was closely watched by the Nazis. He was arrested as an undesirable, and the film was confiscated. Sometime later when Therese made a visit in Eichstätt, a friend excitedly asked her what ever happened to the film. Therese's quick reply was: "Oh, that film was immediately erased and there was nothing on it at all—for them."

On another occasion just before the rise of Hitler, while Therese was suffering the pain of the Passion, her ecstasy and suffering were interrupted while she directed someone at her bedside to inform Father Naber that a man from Berlin was approaching Konnersreuth, and to advise Father not to allow this man to enter the parish house. The messenger relayed this message to Father. It was but a few minutes later when a car with a Berlin license stopped at the rectory. A well-dressed but arrogant man alighted and demanded to see Father Naber regarding an interview that he wished to have with Therese Neumann. Father Naber met him at the rectory door to inform him politely but firmly that no one either at the rectory or at the Neumann residence wished to confer with him. The man returned to his car, cursing and threatening. It was later learned that he was the editor of a Communist newspaper.

One day in February of 1948, Therese had some business to take care of in Tirschenreuth. It was a very bitterly cold day, so she decided to take a taxi from Mitterteich. On the way home, the taxi ran out of gas. The driver was terribly embarrassed; he checked the gas tank, and double-checked by examining the carburetor. There was absolutely no gas in the line, nor in the tank. While the driver spent his time doing that, Therese got out of the car and kept moving, for as she told me, she thought she would freeze to death.

Suddenly, Jesus appeared to Therese and instructed her to have the driver continue the journey. When she told the driver to get in and drive on, he was a little amazed, for how could he drive without gas? Under protest, he got into the car and started the motor. It ran perfectly! The driver just shook his head, for he felt that, as a mechanic, he surely knew when there was no gas in the car. Thoroughly baffled by the situation, he stopped at a house along the way and checked the car once more—contrary to Therese's orders. Now he knew for sure that there was no gas! Thesese directed him to drive on. Again under protest, he did so, and they reached Mitterteich as if nothing had happened. There, at the garage, he could not start the motor any more—there was no gas! The miracle had continued only until Therese had been delivered to her destination.

I once received a picture from a friend of Therese showing a rather large grave marker made of stone; on it was chiseled an angel holding a wreath in his hands and placing it on the head of a small girl. The angel appeared to be coming down through a cloud while the girl was ascending. I wanted an explanation from Father Naber because I was not clear as to its meaning.

He told me that a large family lived right outside Konnersreuth. At one time the father and breadwinner had had a serious illness for a long time. One day, his daughter overheard a conversation between her mother and the doctor; the doctor said there was no hope for her husband and that death might come at any time.

The little girl was so overcome with sadness that she left the house immediately and ran to the home of Therese to ask for help. Therese was very sympathetic toward the girl and tried to comfort her in every way she could, telling her that our ways are not always God's ways. The little girl insisted that it was too sad that Daddy would have to die—and what would happen to her mother and the children; that it would be much better if she, herself, could die in Dad's place. Therese offered the girl her own sufferings for the man. Then she told her to go back home because Mother might be looking for her. The little girl left for home.

A short while after this visit, Therese fell into an ecstasy, which lasted only a few minutes. She saw the heavens open up, and a beautiful angel wearing a pure white garment and bearing a wreath in his hands came through the clouds, placing the wreath on the little girl as she was taken up into Heaven. Therese woke up and had a few minutes of exalted rest, as usual. She told her folks what had happened.

Shortly after the vision, the sad news arrived that the little girl had collapsed while entering her home and had died immediately. Not much time elapsed before the whole story became sensational, as the father was cured immediately upon the death of his daughter. He lived for many years and died a normal death. This prompted the family to place that most appropriate marker on the grave of their little girl. It was designed just as Therese had described the vision.

The day Cardinal Pacelli was to be crowned as Pope Pius XII, Father Naber told Therese to get some friends together in his rectory to listen to the coronation ceremonies from St. Peter's on the radio. They all listened intently for hours. When the time came and the new pope gave his blessing *"urbi et orbi"*—to the city (Rome) and to the world—Therese suddenly fell into ecstasy; her arms were outstretched, and her chair—with Therese in it—suddenly turned around, facing south. Even though all were accustomed to so many unusual happenings, this one came as a complete surprise. When Therese came back to normal after the exalted rest period, she told them that she had, indeed, been right there by the Holy Father and had seen all the people around him.

On one occasion Father Naber visited a friend in Berlin. There he said Mass each morning in a nearby church. When he got back to Konnersreuth, Therese described the church and its contents precisely, and also the conversations Father Naber had had with people he met while in Berlin. Therese had indeed been present in that city through bilocation.

Therese once told me about the many lectures which I give (usually in California). Shocked, I asked her "how in the Sam Hill" she knew that. Without any further to-do she said, "I usually stand right at the door and listen to you." I regret very much that I did not follow through and ask how many times she did that.

Freiherr von Aretin, a German nobleman and author who was famous all over Europe and a longtime friend of Therese, was told by her that the Gestapo would search his house within a few days. In two days, the Gestapo came and searched his home, just as she had foretold.

One morning after Mass, Therese fell into ecstasy right in the sacristy, which was very unusual. She was standing up with her arms fully outstretched toward the ceiling. Suddenly, her two hand wounds were filled with light, almost like a lighted light bulb. Someone was able to take a picture of it and I have seen that picture several times.

On several occasions Therese saw and participated in the ordination of priests in the cathedral in Eichstätt. In ecstasy she saw the Holy Ghost come down upon these newly ordained in the form of *"lebendiges Licht,"* or living light. Also, she was present in her mystical way when Rev. Dr. Joseph Schröffer and Rev. Dr. Rudolf Gräber were consecrated as Bishops in the Roman Catholic Church. But this time, she talked of a living light that was even more brilliant than before. In the case of Dr. Rudolf Gräber, Therese forecast years previously that he one day would be appointed Bishop of Regensburg. She was right. Another time she had a visit with Father Michael Rackl. At that time this priest was rector of the diocesan seminary in Eichstätt. To his surprise, Therese gave him the news that someday he would be Bishop of Eichstätt. Not too much thought was given to this prediction. Years later, Bishop Leo of that city died and Count Conrad von Preysing was appointed Bishop of Eichstätt. Everyone seemed to think of disregarding Therese's prediction, and it was almost forgotten. Three years went by and the Holy Father in Rome appointed Bishop von Preysing to the see of Berlin, where he later became Cardinal. To the surprise of all—except Therese—Father Michael Rackl became Bishop of Eichstätt. Again, Therese was right.

Therese's mystical gifts proved to be a very powerful influence on many. For example, in the late 1920's and 30's a rather frequent visitor to Konnersreuth was Bishop Schrembs of Cleveland, Ohio. I understand that his birthplace was Bavaria. He was therefore in an excellent position to gain superior knowledge of Therese's life since there was no language barrier, as there was with non-German-speaking visitors.

As Bishop Schrembs pointed out in many open discussions, Therese told him of numerous problems in his diocese. She went into perfect detail and also told the Bishop how to make corrections. I recall having heard of the case of his school system in Cleveland, and how Therese told him everything in detail. On one occasion, the mystic recommended that the Bishop cut his visit short in Bavaria because he was badly needed for certain reasons back home. According to Bishop Schrembs, Therese told him things on many occasions that no living person could possibly have known except himself and God. Even on the Bishop's first visit to Konnersreuth, Therese immediately told him who he was and where he was from. She described various characteristics of some of his priests and warned him against certain false friends. She counseled him on the affairs of his diocese, on his duties as a bishop, and made for him what amounted to a regular examination of conscience. The good Bishop was so overcome by the interview that he burst into tears.

Therese received many letters from all over the world. When

she was in her normal state, she opened them and looked at the signatures. She knew the contents immediately, regardless of the language in which the letter was written. If mail was placed near her during an ecstasy, or if her hand was placed on a letter, she knew its contents immediately without opening it.

Therese was chosen as godmother for her sister's daughter. During the baptismal ceremony in the church, conducted by Father Naber, the mystic fell into an ecstasy. The guardian angel of the baby appeared to Therese and told her that the child would be a God-fearing person all her life. This little girl was Benedikta Härtl, who is seen in pictures in this book.

One time in the late fall of 1950, I picked up enough courage and asked Father Naber the question: Has Therese Neumann made any prophecies of any sort during ecstasy or bilocation, etc.? Father Naber was not surprised to get this question from me, and he very kindly told me: Mr. Vogl, nothing can be said about any prophecies coming from Therese, period. And after some pause, he said that any such statements would definitely not be for the use of the general public. Rather, they would be forwarded in a secret memorandum to the Bishop of Regensburg and from there to the proper Vatican authorities. In conclusion, any form of sensationalism in any form was definitely out of the question with both Therese and Father Naber; and Ferdinand Neumann, Sr. (Therese's father) concurred in this. That covers a lot of ground, but it was definitely not being tolerated. From then on, any inquiry about future happenings was for me also a closed subject. Other than that, they always served me in all matters—so much so, that I would never be able to tell all.

— *Chapter 11* —

THERESE'S DAILY ACTIVITIES, DAILY SUFFERINGS, AND PERSONALITY

Therese was always busy, and every minute during the day was taken up with one or the other of many duties and cares. She worked in the church, in the parish house, as well as within and around her own home. The number and variety of these activities were the more remarkable when considered along with the heavy physical demands made upon her by her life as a stigmatist. Actually, very few hours of Therese's day were spent in the state of normal human life, as she had many visions and many special sufferings.

A good deal of Therese's time was spent taking care of the flowers which were used to beautify the altars in the church, the parish house and her own home. The graves in the cemetery were carefully and lovingly tended, and her skill and taste in decorating both the church and the cemetery were a source of gratitude and pride to the townspeople and of edification to visitors. It was not unusual for Therese to spend all night in the village church decorating the altars. The church was always immaculately clean and beautifully decorated, thanks to Therese's tireless devotion.

When the church was to be redecorated some years ago, Therese was entrusted with the direction of this work by universal consent of the people of Konnersreuth, and she accordingly gave all the instructions to the workmen and painters regarding details and color. She designed the beautiful grotto honoring Our Lady which stands inside the main entrance of the church. Father Naber, realizing that the Lord often made His wishes known through Therese, asked her to assume responsibilities of this kind, always with results that were a joy to all.

Therese could be found working in the kitchen, waiting on guests at mealtime, working in the garden, or caring for animals in the stable. She had to spend much time doing work to help her family. She was always obedient to her parents. She did all the work that a housewife would do, and was very efficient, strong and diligent in everything she touched.

Then too, she loved to work out in the field, in the few acres that her dad owned. That was a special joy for her; she could use her strength, and she loved to work her horses and other animals. She had a really good time doing either housework or farm work, but she particularly enjoyed farm work. That came first as far as manual work was concerned; she told me that several times. It was amusing to see her driving to a neighboring village in her cart, drawn by a horse which had been given to her by American soldiers—many of whose buddies owed their lives to the foreknowledge Therese had had of a vicious shelling that could otherwise have caught soldiers and townspeople in the streets. (See Chapter 12.)

The care of her birds was another daily chore which Therese enjoyed. She received birds from all over the world, and she had many rare species. She had an uncanny insight in caring for them, and if we may judge from their full-throated singing, she kept them all very happy.

Of course, Therese had to spend much time with Father Naber at the parish residence, receiving visitors. Notable persons came by the hundreds, often in one week. These visitors included Cardinals, Bishops, priests, nuns and brothers, doctors, lawyers, professors, statesmen, etc. Therese also wrote many letters, despite the fact that this task caused pain in her hand wounds. Between 1952 and 1962 alone, she wrote over 1,500 letters.

Therese spent many hours comforting and assisting the sick and needy. She helped scores of displaced persons and other victims of the horrors and destruction of war. All donations that were given to her were used to help the destitute and the afflicted.

She sent food packages under an assumed name to people in East Germany. The parcels would never have reached their destination with her own name on them. The monetary value of the food distributed by Therese, particularly between the years 1945-1950, would run into six-digit figures. Therese had to use the assumed name because the Hitler regime hated her with a passion. The SS was always in the forefront of hatred of anything Catholic. They had orders to make life as miserable as possible for her, without harming her bodily. There would have been an uprising had she been harmed.

Most generous acts of mercy and love for her fellow beings were also demonstrated by Therese in caring for and feeding sick people in and around the area of Konnersreuth. This small village with a population of about 1,000 had no medical doctor and no hospital until 1947. A horse-drawn carriage was her means of reaching the sick and disabled. As mentioned above, the U.S. GI's had found out about her love of animals and given her a horse. She had a little cart, and the joy she had with that was indeed great.

Everything Therese did in her daily life was done for the love of God. Her deeds of charity and kindness were endless. Therese made reparation to her brother August, who had lived in the home place. Enough ground was purchased near the cemetery so that he could continue farming and live comfortably with his wife and family in a nice home. Therese kept little for herself; she was born poor and she died poor.

From the year 1919 Therese Neumann offered up her suffering to Our Lord for the souls in Purgatory, as well as for the spiritually and physically sick all over the world—and she did so to her last day. It was not unusual for her to suffer for a particular soul detained in Purgatory. This suffering often lasted for days. During this time she had much physical pain to endure, along with anguish of soul. Sustained prayers were offered up for the early release of the afflicted soul. Quite frequently, in a consoling vision, the person for whom she had been suffering and praying appeared to her in glory. She recognized these souls, and knew the difference between the ones from Purgatory and the ones from Heaven.

Additional periods of suffering were endured for the living who may either have been in great spiritual distress or suffering some severe physical affliction. The despondent and despairing who were tempted to suicide were frequent objects of her solicitude, and while helping these through their crises she sometimes had the most agonizing convulsions, during which her body writhed in pain and her own life seemed seriously endangered.

Therese's sufferings were more frequent and severe than most people imagine. She may have suffered several times during the day, and she had asked the Master to permit her to suffer especially for the following: the poor souls in Purgatory; the sick; the dying; people in accidents; would-be suicides; conversions; and for the return of people to the Faith. Therese would suffer many times daily for people all over the world who had asked Our Lord in prayer to tell Therese that they needed help.

Therese voluntarily took upon herself these sufferings in order to alleviate the heavy crosses of her fellow men. This was considered by her spiritual advisers to be a saintly and heroic act of mercy, far beyond the scope of an average Christian. She asked Our Lord that all these sufferings which she took upon herself voluntarily should be credited for the forgiveness of sins for others, and not for herself and her own shortcomings.

Having been with her so many days, my wife and I both agree that Therese Neumann seemed to suffer ailments that are quite common among the population of Bavaria, where the weather is usually cold, and not too warm even in summer. Then, too, the illnesses of the Neumann brothers and sisters were all about alike; these included coronary heart problems. And, of course, rheumatism did bother Therese quite a bit even in 1950. (Keep in mind that she lived only on the Sacred Host from 1922 on—this also means she took no medicines.)

Therese became a member of the Third Order of St. Francis of Assisi on September 2, 1946. When she became a member, the Provincial General from Munich, Father Stanislaus, O.F.M. Cap., came to Eichstätt especially to conduct the ceremonies. Father Naber and Therese's sister Ottilie also became members of the order. On October 17, 1947, during the annual parish mission in Konnersreuth, Therese made her final vows in the presence of the Bavarian Provincial of the Capuchin Order, Father Felix Maria, O.F.M. Cap.

Worthy of note is the fact that Therese Neumann was a frequent visitor at the famous shrine of St. Walburga in Eichstätt, which shrine is in the care of the sisters at the adjacent Benedictine Abbey. Therese would usually go to the abbey on her frequent trips to see Father Wutz and her sister Ottilie, his housekeeper. Therese enjoyed being with these sisters (there were about 100) and she was a personal friend of the abbess.

The shrine is famous for the phenomenon of the "Walburga oil," a phenomenon which has taken place for over 1,200 years. Every year since 870 (the year of the transfer of St. Walburga's relics) a clear liquid flows from the bones of the saint beginning on October 12 and ending on February 25. Over the centuries people have received cures and other favors through the application of this oil; the number of these favors granted to date runs into the thousands. The Benedictine sisters have charge of distributing this miraculous oil. Therese Neumann was an ardent believer in the miracles of the holy oil.

Therese was indeed a very, very happy, joyful person. She also had a very good sense of humor. I recall the time in September of 1950 when my four-year-old son Frankie was playing downstairs with the garden hose with Therese's niece and nephew. Frankie got all wet and I was about to paddle him—but Therese suddenly picked him up and guarded him and told me and Esther that it was not his fault that the water was wet!

Therese often gave away holy cards, and she also wrote spiritual greetings on each one—for instance: "In holy prayer united," "Gladly all sufferings for You, dear Saviour," "Saviour, always faithful to You," "Mary, our good Mother, do not forget us"—and the story goes on and on. Over the years she must have given away thousands of holy cards, mostly one at a time, and each card had a beautiful verse, all written in her own handwriting. Before we left Eichstätt for Altötting during the last days of September, 1950, she handed me a pack of holy cards with at least five different spiritual verses.

Driving through the countryside she was often very happy when we passed a church that was freshly painted. The opposite was true when buildings that house the Lord were not kept up the way she wanted it done. Every day and all times were devoted to her *"Heiland,"* Saviour, and to *"unsere liebe Mutter Gottes,"* our dear Mother of God. Therese also referred to the Blessed Mother as *"Himmelmutter,"* Heavenly Mother, and at other times as *"Mutter Gottes von Altötting."*

To me she preferred to say many things in the Bavarian dialect. I knew it as well as she did, and she got a kick out of the fact that an American could be so genuinely Bavarian. Incidentally, although I could have called Therese by her nickname, "Resl," in Bavarian politeness I always called her "Fräulein Theres," in accord with the local custom. Father Naber I always called "Herr Pfarrer" (Mr. Pastor), which is the Bavarian form of respectful address for priests.

On the occasion when we went to Altötting to the shrine and also to visit my aunts and uncles, we were an hour late for the visit; but Therese ordered me to stop at the shrine first, with me at her side. We were in the shrine at least 30 minutes, and the church was packed, but we managed to wrangle ourselves right up to the black statue of the Madonna of Altötting. What a joy that was for Therese I cannot put down in words. I know, because I was at her side. So that Therese would not be detected, Father Naber, Esther and the relatives had to stay in the car. Of course the stop at the shrine made us even later, but for Therese, Our Lord and His Blessed Mother *always* came first.

Therese was always very solicitous about the human welfare

of her visitors. Indeed, she was able to chat with great talent about everything. She always stunned me with her knowledge of things she would be expected to know little about. She loved to talk about flowers and about farm animals, particularly horses. The flowers she called and knew by their Latin names—I know she did not learn that in her seven years at the little school in Konnersreuth!

Whenever the time came to leave after a visit, Therese always opened the door for future visits. She would say, for instance, "Are we going to see you again?" or "When are you coming back to Konnersreuth again?" She and Father Naber were always very relaxed in our company, and we enjoyed every bit of our visits to the fullest extent.

Therese Neumann was always and every minute of the day like a servant to her fellow human beings, and childlike to the uttermost degree. She showed no pride, no superiority, and never looked down on people; she always looked up, always ready to help and to please. She was a number one person, one of the finest I have met in my 78 years on earth. That goes for Father Naber too. I wonder which of the two is the greater saint in Heaven.

— Chapter 12 —

THERESE NEUMANN
AND WORLD WAR II

Within the circle of friends around Therese Neumann there arose a newspaper called *Der Gerade Weg* (*The Straight Path*), a publication that stood against the fanatical spirit of evil of that time. The founder of *Der Gerade Weg,* Dr. Fritz Gerlich, had been converted to the Catholic Faith through his acquaintance with Therese Neumann.

The Gestapo's storming of *Der Gerade Weg*'s premises and Dr. Gerlich's arrest and death in Dachau are described in Chapter 22. When open resistance to the Nazi regime was no longer possible, Konnersreuth became a support and a symbol of hope for Catholics—and also for non-Catholics.

The Gestapo did make one attempt to arrest Therese. It was decided to make this attempt during a Friday ecstasy. Two agents of the notorious police were detailed to make the arrest, and they approached the Neumann home at noon. Therese, who was at the height of her suffering, suddenly sprang from her bed, walked down the stairs, and flung the house door open to confront her would-be captors just as they reached for the doorbell. Her pitiable figure, covered with blood, with the evidence of her ordeal vivid in every feature, so awed these harsh men that they turned and hurried away as fast as they could walk.

In 1940 Therese Neumann foretold the downfall of Hitler's regime. This prediction was made at a time when the Nazis were firmly in power. It came true in 1945.

Many friends of Therese Neumann were in the forefront of the fight against Nazism. The labors of Fathers Karl and

Adalbert Vogl, of Dr. Fritz Gerlich, and of Father Ingbert Naab have been described elsewhere in this book, along with the account of what they suffered as a result. Father Ingbert Naab struck a particularly prominent blow against the fanatical spirit of that time with his Open Letter to Adolf Hitler, of which 20 million copies were printed. That important letter is reproduced here in an Appendix, and is most enlightening for all who want to understand the evils of those times. The writing of this letter took colossal courage. Father Naab had to flee from place to place; he suffered much, and finally died in exile.

Incidentally, Therese told me on several occasions how well she thought of the American people for all the help they sent to the starving people after the war. Specifically, she thanked the American people for their help in regard to the millions of homeless and displaced persons. Therese herself did much to alleviate sufferings caused by the war.

Therese was also aware of another great evil, Communism, and she often and very readily spoke about that subject to me.

After World War II, thousands of U.S. Army personnel visited Konnersreuth every week from 1945 until Therese's death in 1962. The GI's came to Konnersreuth by bus, train, cars, etc., from all over the SHEAF command. Their total number was around a half million. Therese often also met high-ranking Army officers.

Just after the war, when I was still in the service, I was able to renew my acquaintance with Therese Neumann and Father Naber. (I had first met them in June of 1927.) It was June 21, 1945. We had a very pleasant visit that lasted over four hours. There was so much to talk about! My uncle, Msgr. Adalbert Vogl, had been executed by the Gestapo just two months before. Therese herself had been through much additional suffering, especially toward the end of the war. She said she wanted to show me her home, which still showed the effects of the shell the Nazis had fired into it. We walked together to her home. We went into the stable, where she told me that not a single animal had been hurt—although the shell had exploded right in the stable. The hole in the wall was at least six feet across.

This visit of June 21, 1945 needs further explanation due to the circumstances in which it took place. As a member of the armed forces attached to the Forward Headquarters of Patton's Third Army, I was assigned to work with a team of CIC agents in the G-2 Section. A few weeks after the war's end, this activity—as far as our team was concerned—was terminated. Soon, we were transferred to the Enemy Documents Section, of which I was a member from that day on.

On or about the 19th of June, 1945, I received an order to fulfill a certain mission which would take me to Eichstätt, and from there to Waldsassen, which is right on the Czechoslovakian border. Knowing this area very well from my earlier days while living in Bavaria, my home state, I knew full well that this mission would take me within six miles of Konnersreuth. Upon conclusion of my official duties I wasted no time in driving to Konnersreuth to find out firsthand what the situation was regarding Therese Neumann, Father Naber and the Neumann family.

As I entered Konnersreuth, I parked my jeep near the parish house and walked over to the church to make a visit there for my own intentions. As I walked out I turned to the left to walk around the church toward the Neumann house. There in the churchyard I saw a lady in a long black dress kneeling close to a flowerbed, with her head turned away from me. Not knowing who it was, I spoke to her in Bavarian dialect, asking for some information—and found to my most pleasant surprise that it was Therese Neumann.

She was overjoyed to see another GI, having been so friendly to the many who had liberated the town and to the many GI visitors during the past month. I re-introduced myself, and that started things rolling in high fashion for me. I shall never forget the happiness and joy radiating from Therese's face to see a long-lost member of the family of one of her best friends. I was cordially invited to walk over to the parish house to see Father Naber and share this joyous day with him and with

Marie, Therese's sister, who was the housekeeper.

I was very happy with the wish of Father Naber and Therese Neumann to make this a friendly homecoming. This visit, as I mentioned before, lasted over four hours. Much of the time was taken up with the news from my family in Altötting. On this day Therese received the first news that my uncle, Msgr. Adalbert Vogl, who was a longtime friend of Konnersreuth, had been executed on April 28th by the Gestapo, along with five other prominent citizens, near the national shrine of Altötting. One must keep in mind that there was little or no communication between Konnersreuth and the outside world due to Gestapo surveillance of Therese Neumann and her followers. The SS were always in the forefront of hatred of anything Catholic. The atmosphere, of course, was now all changed, and the terrible persecution was a thing of the past.

Due to the fact that I was on an official mission, having reports to make for Headquarters, my time was limited. Had it not been for these conditions, I could have found out very valuable information on this day. My inquisitive mind was somewhat uneasy not to have been able to get to what had happened during the fighting in and around Konnersreuth, and what part Therese had played during the takeover by the U.S. liberation army. It was not until 1955 that I had the great luck of getting acquainted with Father Raymond Copeland, S.J., from the University of Santa Clara in California. Here is Father Copeland's report, as he told it to me:

On or a few days after the war's end in May of 1945, the unit of which he was the Catholic chaplain liberated Konnersreuth. Having heard of Therese Neumann and Konnersreuth, he took the first opportunity to report to the local priest—who was, of course, Father Naber. Through an interpreter, arrangements were quickly made to have a meeting between Therese and some of his men. They had a very delightful visit and it was agreed that Father Copeland would celebrate Mass in the church at 5 p.m. that day.

Father Copeland was so enthusiastic about the wonderful meeting that he instructed his jeep driver to park his vehicle within sight of the church and take some pictures as he left the church with Therese and Father Naber. The plan worked perfectly; Father Copeland was happy about this because he wanted some nice pictures of the occasion. A few days later, after the pictures were developed, he found that all the others came out perfectly—but all that were taken of Therese were complete blanks! It was very common during the years of Therese Neumann that this sort of unpleasant thing would happen if pictures were taken without her permission. She was always an opponent of sensationalism, and Our Lord protected her in this way regarding her wishes.

However, on the following day, after Father Copeland celebrated Mass in Konnersreuth for the troops and the townspeople, he and all concerned were indeed allowed to witness and be part of an occurrence which was most unusual and unexplained. (I experienced hundreds myself, and so did my wife when she was with me.)

On this second day of the American GIs' presence in Konnersreuth, Therese had a visit from Our Lord during which she was ordered to inform the men of the Army, as well as the townspeople, very emphatically, that within a certain hour Hitler's Gestapo troops (who were at this time still occupying the forests of the outlying area) would attempt to destroy the city, and that certain precautions had to be taken immediately to minimize the casualties. Therese was told exactly which bunkers should be occupied and which should by all means be avoided.

To the great surprise of Father Copeland and the officers and men, Therese told them of her plan in no uncertain terms. The army went into action to carry out her instructions. The bombardment took place as predicted, with heavy shelling from cannons. All those who were protected by the designated bunkers were saved, including the GIs and others who had received the orders. However, in the confusion and the shortness of time, not all could be informed of this very unusual order. Seventeen houses were completely destroyed, many houses and barns were partially destroyed, and over two dozen lives were lost—but not a single American soldier lost his life.

Another memorable meeting came about for me on May 28, 1945, when I was ordered by Third Army Headquarters to drive to Munich and have an audience with Cardinal Michael von Faulhaber, Archbishop of Munich and Freising. It was in connection with a very important problem which had to be cleared up.

I did what I was told. I had no problem at all in getting in front of a very large line, due to my special pass from General George Patton. I introduced myself, explaining that I was a nephew of Msgr. Adalbert Vogl, a namesake, and that I was now a citizen of the United States and a member of the Third Army. The Cardinal was flabbergasted, and also was pleased to have a GI speak to him in native Bavarian.

After discussion of the execution of my dear uncle, who had been a longtime personal friend of His Eminence, I proceeded with my mission. After this was all done properly, I made it a point to tell the Cardinal that I was to bring him greetings from Therese Neumann, whom I had met earlier in Konnersreuth. He expressed his concern about her and I informed him that all was finally well. Upon my questions to him regarding Therese he told me that he always stood behind her. In fact, he said, "I regard myself as a longtime personal friend of this holy suffering soul." He mentioned that I might know how often he had even used her holy life in his sermons in the Cathedral of St. Michael. I responded that I knew quite a bit of that. He then took a picture card from his desk and signed it: Greetings and Blessing, ✛M. Cardinal.

This meeting with Cardinal Faulhaber was a great privilege and a wonderful opportunity for me to hear firsthand a very important "endorsement" of Therese Neumann by this great prelate of the Church in Germany.

Here I will relate a story which, although only indirectly related to Therese Neumann, is nonetheless very important for me because through these events I had the opportunity of spending three to four hours discussing Therese Neumann

with Rt. Rev. Willibald Mangraf, O.S.B., Abbot of the
Benedictine Abbey of Schweikelberg and a member of the
German Bishops' Conference. This story was also told to
Therese Neumann, Father Naber and Mr. Ferdinand Neu-
mann during a visit in 1953; they were all delighted with
it and I received compliments for having been involved in it.

The date was approximately July 25, 1945. I was stationed
at the Third Army Intelligence Center at Freising, Bavaria
as a member of the Int. G-2 Section. On that day I received
an assignment from Headquarters to proceed with my jeep
to the Benedictine Abbey at Schweikelberg. The Abbey was
located high up on a hill overlooking the city of Vilshofen
and the Danube River—indeed a very beautiful setting.

With my equipment in the trailer I arrived at the Abbey
in about two hours. I asked one of the brothers for the Abbot;
he obliged and I was soon speaking to Rt. Rev. Willibald
Mangraf. I showed him my credentials and why I was sent
there. The Abbot was very kind to me and obviously pleased
that the U.S. Army was finally doing something to correct
a very deplorable condition.

I soon found out that it was indeed a typical diabolical
Nazi deed that I had to correct. I was used to that. According
to Father Abbot, the Hitler SS had taken over the Abbey
with the intention of making it into a special SS training
school. Therefore the seminary was eliminated, the monks
with few exceptions were sent off into the unknown, and the
beautiful abbey church was used as a warehouse with furniture stored not less than 6 ft. high—and sometimes 10 ft.
To my knowledge there were only four or five monks left
when I got there. All the seminarians were gone. One section of the Abbey had been used as a German Army hospital.
There was no church (only a chapel for the few monks).
Obviously, if Hitler had won the war the Abbey would today
be an Elite School of the SS.

That was what I found. After two days of planning I told
Father Abbot that I would report on the situation to my superiors in Friesing, that I would ask for a tough and able

member of my section to help me with this big problem, and that I would be back in a day. I chose a sergeant from New York whose name was Robert. He was Jewish, I was Catholic. That was a natural team to clean out a Nazi mess.

On arrival in Schweikelberg I told Robert that the first thing he had to do was drive down to Vilshofen and request three or four MP's from the U.S. military commander—upon orders from Third Army Headquarters; they would have to supply prisoners from the local SS compound and march them up to the Abbey every day to clear out the big church. This would have to be done until the job was finished.

Everything went as I had planned. The prisoners were treated very humanely. I had them fed and they were allowed normal rest periods like those we were accustomed to during our training.

On or about August 9th the beautiful church was cleared of everything that had been stored in it for years. The prisoners also had to help with the cleaning-up process; they co-operated with me to the fullest extent. The church was then ready to be re-blessed and properly decorated for the upcoming Feast of the Assumption, August 15th. All this was done in a most joyful mood, and all concerned were grateful to Almighty God that the good had again overcome the evil.

Several interesting details are worth sharing with my readers. During my stay at the Abbey for about fourteen days I had numerous occasions to talk to the Father Abbot regarding the life of Therese Neumann. He was very well-informed on all that and also shared his views with me very readily. I thank Father Abbot yet today for all the information he gave me, which has helped enable me to write about Therese Neumann as I do. The other monk I dealt with used to be the organist; he was anxiously watching the progress of clearing the church so that he could get to his organ (which was all covered) and get it ready for the high feastday. I cannot find words to express the joy of these monks, as well as that of the sisters from across the street, and their appreciation for what the Yankees had done for them.

During the fourteen days I worked at the Abbey with my co-worker Robert, we got into most of the chambers of the monastery. One day we accidentally ran into a large storage place filled with new toilets, wash basins, all kinds of plumbing, shower equipment and lots of ceramic tile. I reported this to the Abbot and he told me that that was all intended for the new Elite Hitler SS school which was to be opened after the war. Robert and I started laughing loudly and we informed the Abbot that from now on it was the official property of the Benedictine seminary which was to be re-opened, hopefully soon.

During my time at the monastery I had one room for myself. I decided to eat with the sisters across the street. They were taking care of displaced persons. I gave them my U.S. rations and enjoyed eating with the poor people morning, noon and night. The sisters waited on us. One day a sister came up to me (of course I was "king") and asked me how come I spoke the Bavarian dialect as well as they did. I told her if you tell me where you come from in Bavaria, then I will tell where I come from. That was a deal. She said her name was Sister Conradine, O.S.B.; she was born a Sendlinger in Arbing and had been a sister for quite some time. I threw my arms around her and kissed her. She was my cousin from my mother's side and we used to play together in our early youth.

I have been back at Schweikelberg five times. A visit was made there with my wife and son Frank in 1950. At that time the Rev. Father Abbot was still active. He gave me his photograph and wrote on the back:

In Remembrance! Your thankful
✝Willibald Mangraf
Abbot of Schweikelberg
August 8, 1950

In 1957 I met four American priests in Bavaria. They were Fathers Wilkiemeyer from Santa Clara, Monahan and Kennedy from San Francisco and Wilkiemeyer (brother of the afore-mentioned) from Oklahoma City. On our way back from Kon-nersreuth I drove my guests up to the Abbey. We stayed there overnight and were greeted and treated royally by the Abbot. At the breakfast table the next day I translated my discussion for the guests. It was regarding Therese Neumann—who else! Again it was all good news for me as well as my co-travelers.

Right after breakfast Rev. Father Abbot suggested that he take me and the four priests down to the lower floor of the Abbey. We were then shown the newly installed shower, bath-room and washrooms which were already in use for the semi-narians.

We then took leave of that beautiful and sacred place.

— *Chapter 13* —

INVESTIGATION BY THE CHURCH

In 1927, Archbishop Michael Buchberger of Regensburg directed that a study be made of the physical condition of Therese Neumann and the unusual phenomena surrounding her life. He received the wholehearted support of Therese, the Neumann family, and Father Naber. The order was given to conduct this investigation from Thursday, July 14, to Thursday, July 28, 1927. The Bishop requested four sisters from the convent in Mallersdorf, Bavaria, to assist in the study. They were under oath and were responsible to the Bishop; they were to report their findings to him. These sisters were trained nurses and came from such medical departments as surgery, x-ray and dentistry. One was adept at shorthand and thus recorded not only her own observations, but those of the others as well. At the request of the Archbishop of Regensburg, a professor of the Federal Psychiatric Research Clinic of the University of Erlangen, Dr. Ewald, M.D., a non-Catholic, was appointed director of the fifteen-day investigation. Another prominent physician, a Catholic, Dr. Seidl from Waldsassen, Bavaria, was to be Dr. Ewald's close collaborator. As in the case of the four sisters, all of whom were trained nurses, the doctors, too, were under oath and responsible to the Archbishop of Regensburg.

The rules of the investigation were as follows:

1. The sisters were to work in two shifts, two sisters in each. All occurrences were to be recorded on paper.
2. Therese was not to be left alone, day or night.
3. She was to be bathed with a damp cloth; a sponge, which might have held some water, was prohibited.

4. Water used in cleaning her teeth had to be measured before and after.

5. The amount of water used to enable her to swallow the Host was to be measured.

6. Any bodily discharges were to be carefully reserved for measurement and chemical analysis. [After 1930 Therese had *no* natural eliminations from her body—including urination, stool and menstruation.]

7. Temperature and pulse were to be checked periodically each day.

8. The blood shed during her sufferings was to be carefully caught, measured and analyzed.

9. Very accurate and detailed descriptions were to be recorded in writing of the bleeding periods during the Friday ecstasies.

10. The cloths used to cover the head and heart wounds were to be saved.

11. Photographs were to be taken of the stigmata and, circumstances permitting, also of various phases of the ecstasies.

12. Observations and recordings were to extend to Therese's religious life, as well as to her behavior toward her family and visitors.

13. Dr. Seidl was to remain immediately available, to enable the sisters to relate their observations with technical accuracy and to clear up any questions of the relevancy and significance of what was observed.

This investigation was conducted by the four nursing sisters, who were all under oath—a fact which places their testimony beyond all reasonable doubt. The report of this investigation was examined by Dr. Ewald and by Dr. Seidl, who turned it over to the Archbishop of Regensburg. The report to the Bishop was placed under protocol, to be used at the proper time.

Since the Archbishop never ordered another investigation, we may rest assured that if the slightest suspicion had arisen from this investigation, a ban would have immediately stopped all Catholics from visiting Therese at Konnersreuth.

Prof. Dr. Ewald, the consulting medical adviser to Dr. Seidl, gave high praise to the sisters, and said that no investigation could have been conducted more honestly and with more precision. He spoke of Therese's total abstinence from food and of the fact that she never demonstrated any urge to eat. The total amount of water consumed by Therese when receiving Communion during the investigation was 45cc., or about two tablespoonsful. Her actual discharge was measured as being 345cc. One of the most surprising observations was that of her weight:

```
July  13—55   kg. (121   lbs.)
July  16—51   kg. (112.2 lbs.)
July  20—54   kg. (118.8 lbs.)
July  23—52.5 kg. (115.5 lbs.)
July  28—55   kg. (121   lbs.)
```

I have had several discussions with medical men regarding the weight differences. I have been told that anyone losing five pounds of weight while fasting, and wishing to gain that back within eight days, would have to eat eight times five pounds, or forty pounds of food. Therese regained more than this much weight in only two days—without eating or drinking!

Now the question: Did Therese Neumann refuse further investigations? The answer is: Neither Therese, her family, nor Father Naber refused any request coming from the proper ecclesiastical authorities. They gladly complied with every request made by the Church. (And besides inquiries made under Catholic auspices, investigations were made by Protestant and Jewish experts who had become genuinely interested in the phenomenon of Konnersreuth and were permitted to make tests and record their findings).

But with regard to examinations requested by other than Catholic Church authorities, there had to be a limit. If Therese were to have entered one clinic for examination, how could other clinics have been refused the same privilege? The results of more investigations would only have been a tedious repetition of those already conducted. Therese's father had a perfect right not to permit his daughter to be subjected to sensationalism and curiosity.

On several occasions Mr. Neumann received mysterious communications to the effect: "If we could only have Therese in our clinic, we would give her 'clinical observation' she would not forget for a long time!" Can you blame a faithful father for refusing to subject his daughter to such indignities and exploitations parading under the disguise of "scientific investigations"?

But if the Archbishop of Regensburg, or any higher ecclesiastical authority, wanted to have a series of tests or observations conducted by accredited medical experts, neither Therese nor Mr. Neumann nor Father Naber would have refused. They would all have cooperated in every possible way. Each of them assured me of this most emphatically. What they wished to avoid was a recurrence of the regrettable experience involving Dr. Deutsch. (See Chapter 24).

There is no doubt that the report of the investigation of July, 1927 was turned over to the Archbishop of Regensburg. Moreover, it is my personal opinion that the reports of many private investigations dealing with the language phenomenon and with Therese's physical condition and visions were made available to the Archbishop and to the Vatican. Many priests in Bavaria have told me that the Vatican is very well informed on all the occurrences in Konnersreuth.

In fact, Pope Pius XI requested Professor Gemelli, an eminent medical scientist and rector of the University of the Sacred Heart in Milano, Italy, to be present in Konnersreuth for the Friday ecstasies of March 23 and April 6, 1928, and to make a report to him personally. Prof. Gemelli conducted these investigations, and it became common knowledge later that the reports which he made were favorable to Therese Neumann. Before Prof. Gemelli left Konnersreuth the second time, he mentioned to Therese that he was due in the Vatican on a certain day. To his surprise, she told him that he could not possibly make it on that day. But he knew his schedule, and could not understand why his plan would be changed. Later, he wrote Therese that she had been right! He had had a mishap, and had arrived in Rome just when she had said he would.

Pope Pius XI maintained a keen interest in Therese Neumann from the time she was first brought to his attention until his death in 1939. He was frequently informed of the happenings at Konnersreuth. He showed his favorable attitude toward her and his mild impatience with her detractors by exclaiming: "*Lässt mir das Kind in Ruhe!*" (Leave the child alone!) On one occasion Pope Pius XI sent Therese a personal gift of a very precious relic of St. Francis of Assisi.

On May 3, 1928, Therese was transported in a vision to the office of the Holy Father in the Vatican. She stood behind the Pope and watched him sign two papers. On one she recognized the name of Father Naber, and on the other her own name. After the vision she went quickly to tell Father Naber what she had seen. He marked the date on his calendar. About fourteen days later, a courier of the papal nuncio in Munich delivered these two papers; they were the Holy Father's personal blessings for Father Naber and Therese Neumann!

Pope Pius XII continued the same paternal interest in Therese that was displayed by his predecessor. He sent her a very precious relic. He also sent his blessing to her many times; my wife and I were present on one occasion when Therese received a message from the Holy Father. It happened in mid-September, 1950 when, accompanied by my wife, I drove Therese and Father Naber to Munich to visit Dr. Mittendorfer.

When we arrived, we learned that Therese's brother, Ferdinand, in company with his wife and a friend, would also come for a visit. At that time, Ferdinand was a member of the Bavarian Parliament. When he and his wife and their friend, a journalist, arrived, we were introduced to all of them. The journalist told Therese that he had just returned from the Holy Year observances in Rome, where he had gone with a group of other German journalists. He told her he had a very important message for her: "When our group of newspaper men were received in a private audience by Pope Pius XII, the Holy Father spoke to each of us in German. When he came to me, he asked: 'Where are you from?' I said, 'From near Konnersreuth.' 'Ah,' said the Holy Father, 'Do you, by chance, know Therese Neumann?' 'Yes,' I replied. The Pope then said, 'Will you give her my very best regards when you see her?' " The journalist assured the Holy Father that he would convey the message to Therese at the earliest opportunity. We were fortunate enough to be present when this request was carried out. Therese was very happy, and of course we all shared her joy with her!

The topic of investigation of Therese Neumann is not complete unless I refer to the proposed investigation in 1937. At that time the Hitler regime was running rampant. All the Catholic youth organizations were eliminated, priests had to have their Sunday sermons censored, and many priests were put in concentration camps. This was also the fate of many Catholic lay leaders. In short, things were going from bad to worse as the months went by. One very diabolical aspect of the persecution against anti-Nazis was the fact that once you were put into a concentration camp, or under Nazi jurisdiction, you were broken in mind and body. Today we know even more of what adversaries do; just let me mention Cardinal Mindszenty and Bishop Walsh. The prisoners of Hitler fared just as badly.

It was under these circumstances that a simple, ordinary Christian could not understand that people near the Vatican thought they could satisfy their curiosity by asking the authorities for another examination of Therese Neumann. This would have meant that Therese would be put in a Nazi clinic where she could very likely be permanently ruined in health and mind. At best, she would have been handled like an enemy of the state—and we all know what that implied in 1937. I mention this in order to let people know, once and for all, that this request did not come from the Vatican, but from certain elements in Rome. This request, since it did come from Rome but was not official, came to the attention of the Apostolic Delegate, Gustav Testa.

There is a letter on file dated January 20, 1937, written by the Apostolic Delegate in Munich and directed to the Assessor of the Holy Office in the Vatican, Msgr. Ottaviani (later Cardinal). This letter says in no uncertain terms that, considering the condition of the times, Therese Neumann should be spared another medical examination. The very unexpected suggestion for additional tests on Therese also came to the attention of the Bishop of Regensburg and to the Bishop of Eichstätt, who was at that time Conrad von Preysing (later the Cardinal of Berlin). Their decision was a unanimous "NO." Under no circumstances should Therese be put into the hands of Nazi doctors. Joining in this decision were many Catholic educators and non-Catholics as well.

When we speak of investigations regarding the most unusual occurrences in the life of Therese, we must say, in all truthfulness, that her whole life was closely watched by doctors on a daily basis. Her whole life consisted of a continuous watching and investigating by standby doctors of her own family and many others who came from far away. These medical men included not only Catholics, but also non-Catholic and Jewish doctors as well. Many doctors who were allowed to examine Therese belonged to no religion at all, and it is known that some were unbelievers.

I wanted to check this out further on one of my visits, and I had a long talk with a theology professor who had known Therese very well for many years. I asked, "How many times, or how often do you think Therese was checked by individual doctors, other than the known official investigation?" He asked me in return, "How often do you think this was the case?" I hazarded a guess of about 500 times. Then he replied that although he did not know the exact number of times, he thought my guess was too low. Some of these were investigations ordered by Father Naber, with the permission of Therese's parents.

Therese and the Neumann family, with the knowledge of Father Naber, gave permission for this in order to establish the facts of all the happenings of her unusual medical life. We humans can do no more nor less to prove such cases on the basis of human knowledge as far as we are able; after we get through investigating, we start all over again and repeat what has been done. This was done in Konnersreuth, starting from Therese's first mystical experiences and the appearance of the stigmata in 1926, and ending with her death in 1962.

What occurred in Konnersreuth with Therese is beyond scientific explanation. Beyond any doubt, it was an act of God, and the fact remains that Therese Neumann was a true mystic and stigmatist of supernatural gifts.

— *Chapter 14* —

CONVERSIONS

It is significant that scores of people have found the True Faith or returned to its practice after visiting Konnersreuth. One of the many notable cases of conversion is that of Bruno Rothschild, a Jew from Vienna. This gentleman happened to read an article about Therese Neumann. He did not know what to think of it. It kept bothering him until he decided to ask a priest what he must do to see Therese.

Bruno Rothschild was not looking for any spectacle or sensation—he was searching for something much greater than either. Yet he knew not where to go, or which way to turn. The kind priest wrote to Father Naber, who gladly granted his request for Bruno to visit Therese.

The succeeding weeks were spent driving back and forth between Vienna and Konnersreuth. Bruno was overwhelmed by what he saw! He saw Therese in her suffering, he saw her wounds bleed, and he experienced the gruesome sight of her physical suffering and apparent death during Friday ecstasies. All this, and so many incidental things one saw and heard when with Therese. Bruno decided to be baptized and to become a Catholic.

During some of the instruction periods, Therese had visions of Bruno's family on their way to Konnersreuth to influence him not to go ahead with his plan. In each case, Bruno left Konnersreuth for awhile, until his family had returned to Vienna.

Bruno later studied for the priesthood and was ordained. Not many years after that, he died from a heart ailment. He is buried in Konnersreuth, which he loved so much. Anyone visiting Konnersreuth should visit his grave. It is just

The Neumann family home in Konnersreuth. The two windows above the lattice are the windows of Therese's room.

Therese's father, Ferdinand Neumann, Sr.

Therese's mother, Anna Neumann. Therese was the first of Anna's eleven children (one of whom died in infancy).

Therese in the early years after receiving the stigmata. This photograph was taken in the rectory of Fr. Wutz in Eichstätt.

Therese Neumann after her stigmatization in the year 1926; the first wounds appeared when she was almost 28 years old.

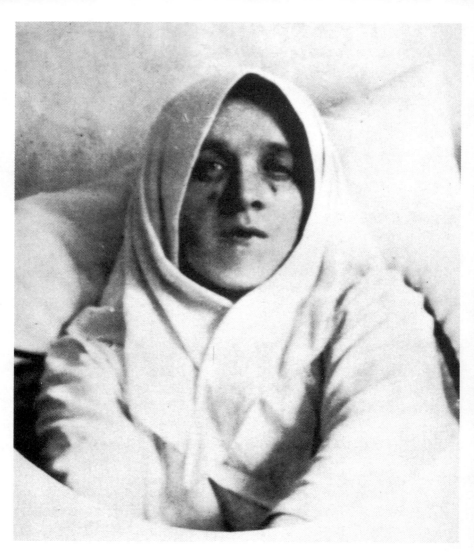

Therese suffering.

Upper: Therese working in the fields. Farm labor was Therese's favorite type of manual labor, and she enjoyed it very much.
Lower: Therese during a Friday suffering of the Passion of Jesus.

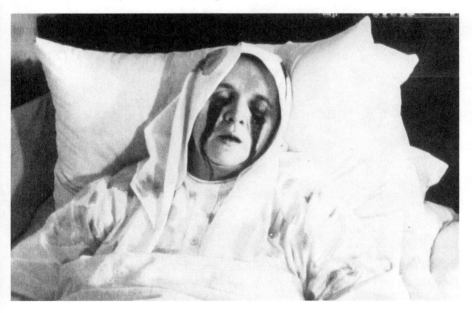

Therese and her flowers; she loved flowers and spent much time tending them and arranging them on the altar at the parish church in Konnersreuth. Since she did not sleep, Therese often used the early hours of the morning to clean the church and decorate it with flowers.

Therese Neumann in 1952; this photograph was taken for an I.D. card.

Upper: The happiness of the children of God reflected in the faces of Father Joseph Naber, Therese's spiritual director for over 50 years, and Therese.
Lower: Therese and Father Naber in the garden of the rectory in Konnersreuth.

Upper: Therese's pony, given to her by American GI's in 1945, after the Liberation.
Lower: Therese with horses. She loved farm animals and took excellent care of them.

Upper: Therese with the pony given to her by the GI's. She loved it dearly, took excellent care of it, and showed it off with great delight to cardinals, bishops, generals and statesmen. *Lower:* Therese holding a tiny chick.

Albert Vogl in Konnersreuth as an American GI in 1945. In the background can be seen the damage from bombing by the German SS; Therese was very happy that the animals in the stable had been spared.

Therese Neumann with Albert Vogl and Fr. Naber in 1945, when Mr. Vogl renewed his acquaintance with Therese.

American GI's lined up in front of the Konnersreuth rectory to visit with Therese Neumann; Therese and Fr. Naber are approaching. War damage can be seen in the background.

Therese and Fr. Naber in a group picture taken in Fr. Sebastian Vogl's garden in Altötting. On the left are the author's wife Esther and young son Frank; also pictured are Albert Vogl's aunts. On the far right is Therese's niece and goddaughter, Benedikta Härtl; at the Baptism Therese saw a vision of the little girl's guardian angel, who told her that Benedikta would always be a God-fearing person.

Group picture taken in Eichstätt in Fr. Wutz's garden in September of 1950. Left to right: Esther Vogl, Therese's sister Ottilie Neumann, Benedikta Härtl, Therese Neumann, Albert Vogl.

Another group picture taken in Fr. Wutz's garden: Benedikta Härtl, Therese, Ottilie, Konrad Härtl (Therese's nephew), and Albert Vogl.

Albert Vogl and Therese's father, Ferdinand Neumann.

Albert Vogl with his Volkswagen near Konnersreuth. At this spot and in this car on October 15, 1953 Therese had a vision of the death of St. Teresa of Avila. Fr. Naber and Albert Vogl were in the front seat and Therese was alone in the back. The ecstasy lasted for a little over 20 minutes. Then, after another 20 minutes of "exalted rest," Therese was back to normal and told her companions all about the vision. (Bro. Krispin, O.F.M. Cap. took this picture.)

The Neumann family and Father Naber.

Upper: Therese having a friendly chat with Abbess Benedikta von Spiegel, Mother Superior of the large Benedictine Abbey of St. Walburga in Eichstätt. These sisters are in charge of the St. Walburga Shrine and St. Walburga Oil. Therese was a frequent visitor to the Abbey. *Lower:* A game of chess between Therese and the Abbess, with another nun and Therese's sister Ottilie looking on.

Therese and the Abbess in the garden of the Abbey, surrounded by a host of Benedictine nuns. In 1986 this abbey had 98 sisters.

Upper: Therese and the Abbess in the Abbey garden.
Lower (left to right): Fr. Ingbert Naab, Therese Neumann, Fr. Wutz, Ottilie Neumann.

The Benedictine Abbey at Schweikelberg, where in 1945 Albert Vogl carried out a U.S. Army assignment to engineer the cleaning out of the Abbey church, which had been used by the Nazis for storage in preparation for turning the Abbey into an elite school for the Hitler SS. (They had expelled the monks.) Mr. Vogl later described this mission to Therese Neumann, Fr. Naber and Therese's father, who heard the story with great satisfaction. Therese too had suffered from the Nazis during World War II. In this picture the city of Vilshofen and the Danube River are visible in the background; beyond them is the beginning of the Bavarian forest.

The Abbey church at Schweikelberg, which had been filled by the Nazis with furniture to a height of 6 - 10 feet. After about 14 days of work, the church was finally cleared out, re-blessed and decorated in time for the Feast of the Assumption, August 15, 1945.

Abbot Willibald Mangraf of the Abbey of Schweikelberg. He and the monks were delighted that the American army had assisted them in clearing out the Abbey church. Albert Vogl had many opportunities to speak with the Abbot about Therese Neumann; he found him very well-informed and favorable toward her.

Fockenfeld Castle near Konnersreuth. Through the prayers and work of Therese Neumann, the Fockenfeld property was purchased in 1951 for a seminary for late vocations. The beautiful property has a long history, with the castle having been built in the 1700's. The complex has been enlarged by subsequent construction. As of Autumn 1986 there had been over 250 priestly ordinations from this seminary.

The Theresianum, a Carmelite convent in Konnersreuth established through the work and prayers of Therese Neumann. This was Therese's last project before her death in 1962. After Therese's death, Mr. Vogl was welcomed to the convent as a guest, and the sisters listened eagerly to his stories about Therese Neumann.

Fr. Naber, Therese's spiritual director for over 50 years. Fr. Naber was unfailingly kind to the throngs of visitors who visited Konnersreuth over the decades, patiently answering the same questions over and over again.

A later picture of Therese, watering her flowers.

Therese Neumann 8 days before her death on September 18, 1962, along with Anni Spiegl (longtime devoted friend of Therese), Anni's daughter and her husband, and Fr. Naber.

Therese 8 days before her death.

Foto Studio Löwenhag, Marktredwitz

Therese Neumann as she lay in state for the public to view shortly before her burial. If in the future the Church should order her grave to be opened, her remains can be compared with this picture at that time.

Cardinal Michael von Faulhaber, Archbishop of Munich (center front) and other clerics. Cardinal Faulhaber was very favorable toward Therese Neumann and used to mention her in the Cathedral of St. Michael in Munich; on one occasion he told a packed church that Therese was "a living tabernacle." To the right of the Cardinal, wearing glasses, is Msgr. F. X. Konrad, pastor of Altötting; next to him is Fr. Ruppert Mayer, S.J., the most decorated army chaplain in World War I and a priest who suffered much at Dachau; Fr. Mayer was beatified by Pope John Paul II in 1987. In the back row, second from the left, is Msgr. Adalbert Vogl, uncle of the author and a good friend of Therese Neumann; Msgr. Adalbert Vogl was executed by the Gestapo.

Michael Kardinal Faulhaber
Erzbischof von München

Carl Pospesch, Salzburg

+ Andreas Rohracher,
Erzbischof v. Salzburg.

hat am _____ 19 _

in *Gruss u. Segen*

an *+ M. Cardinal*

das hl. Sakrament der Firmung
gespendet.

Dies bestätigt: _____

28 May 1945

Left: Handwritten card given to Albert Vogl by Cardinal Faulhaber during an interview.
Regarding Therese Neumann the Cardinal told Mr. Vogl, "I regard myself as a longtime
personal friend of this holy suffering soul."
Right: Archbishop Andreas Rohracher, formerly Archbishop of Salzburg, another strong
and open supporter of Therese Neumann. The Archbishop gave Mr. Vogl this autographed
card in 1973 after an hour-long interview on Therese.

Dr. Mittendorfer, M.D. with Fr. Naber. Dr. Mittendorfer was a medical advisor to Therese for many years. He was always ready to leave his busy practice in Munich to come to Konnersreuth and drive Therese any place she had to go; he dubbed himself "Therese's chauffeur."

Msgr. Adalbert Vogl (*left*) and Msgr. Karl Vogl (*right*), 2 priest uncles of the author through whom he was privileged to become a friend of Therese and the Neumann family. Msgr. Adalbert Vogl was administrator of the national shrine of Bavaria, Our Lady of Altötting; he was publicly executed by the Nazis in April of 1945, just 24 hours before the army of liberation entered Altötting. Msgr. Karl Vogl died a natural death in 1938 after being harrassed by the Gestapo night and day from the very day after the Nazis came to power in 1933. Msgr. Karl Vogl, a personal friend of Cardinal Pacelli (later Pope Pius XII), was founder and chief editor of *Altöttinger Liebfrauenbote* (circulation up to 110,000); he was one of the best-known Catholic journalists in the German-speaking world during the period from 1910-1935. He wrote up the Earling, Iowa exorcism case, which is now published under the title *Begone Satan*. On All Saints Day of 1953 each of these priests appeared to Therese Neumann at age 33 and with a full head of hair, to her amusement and delight.

Upper: Therese Neumann's handwriting and signature in German script on the back of a holy card. It says: "Saviour, faithful to You at all times! In holy prayer united! Therese Neumann."

Lower: Redrawing of a sketch by Dr. Fritz Gerlich based on Therese's description of a Christmas vision.

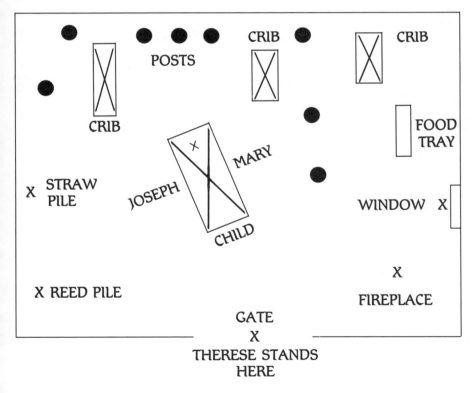

Left: Bishop Rudolf Gräber of Regensburg, who in 1971 ordered Fr. Carl Sträter to open the investigative process on Therese Neumann.

Right: Fr. Carl Sträter, formerly one of the two vice postulators in Therese's cause. (He has since retired.)

Opposite: English translation of the table of contents of the *Positiones et Artikuli,* a document which concludes the informative process on Therese Neumann preparatory to the opening of the actual Cause for Beatification.

CONTENTS

A. Life History of the Servant of God

I. Birth, Home, and Parents

II. In Service

III. The Accident of 10.3.1918 and its Results

IV. The Years of Illness (1918 – 1925)

V. The Healings

VI. The Stigmatisation

VII. The Absence of Nourishment
(The Year of Ecclesiastic Observation, 1927)

VIII. The Time of Restricted Access

IX. The "Occupation" of the Servant of God

X. The Visions of the Servant of God

XI. The Journeys and Visits

XII. The Apoplexy 1940

XIII. The Manner of Living

XIV. The Two Foundations

B. Heroic Virtues

I. The Heroism of All Virtues

II. Heroic Faith

III. Heroic Hope

IV. Heroic Love for God

V. Heroic Love for the Neighbour

VI. Heroic Prudence

VII. Heroic Fortitude

VII. Heroic Justice

IX. Heroic Temperance

X. Heroic Obedience

XI. Heroic Poverty

XII. Heroic Chastity

XIII. Heroic Humility

C. Supernatural Gifts

D. Last Illness and Death of the Servant of God

E. Odour of Sanctity During Life and After Death

F. Miracles After Her Death

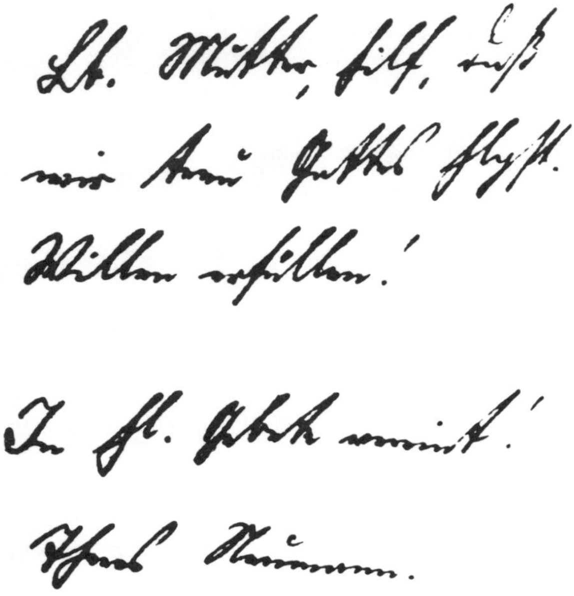

Lb. Mutter, hilf uns, daß
wir treu Gottes hlgst.
Willen erfüllen!

In hl. Gebet vereint!

Therese Neumann.

Inscriptions from the backs of two holy cards. This one says, "Dear Mother, help us to fulfill faithfully God's Holy Will! In holy prayer united! Therese Neumann."

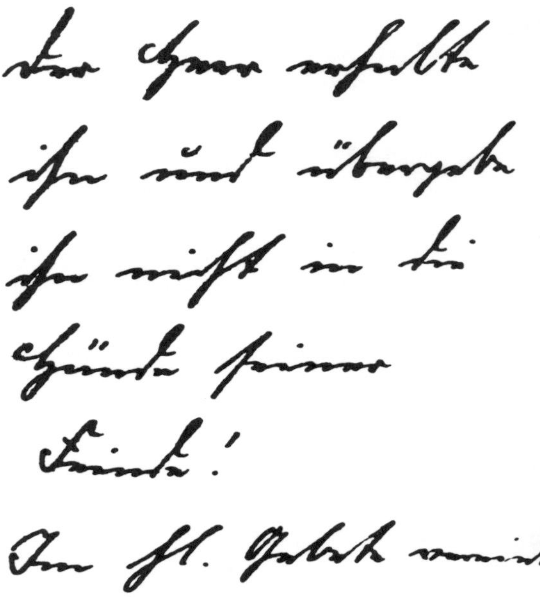

Der Herr erhalte
ihn und übergebe
ihn nicht in die
Hände seiner
Feinde!

In hl. Gebet vereint
Therese Neumann.

[Regarding the Holy Father:] "The Lord keep him and protect him, that he may not fall into the hands of his enemies! In holy prayer united. Therese Neumann."

Drawings of the wounds in the hands of Therese Neumann made to exact size by Albert and Esther Vogl to the best of their ability. These were drawn on the last Friday of September, 1950 after the Vogls had finished a five-day, 600-kilometer vacation trip with Therese Neumann and Father Joseph Naber. Therese Neumann bore these wounds from 1926 until her death in 1962.

Exact size of the wound in Therese Neumann's right hand; it is 1 centimeter long.

Exact size of the wound in Therese Neumann's left hand; it is 1 1/2 centimeters long.

~~~~~~

This drawing of the heart wound of Therese Neumann was done by Dr. Fritz Gerlich of Munich and given to the author's uncle, Msgr. Adalbert Vogl of Altötting. Therese Neumann bore this wound too from 1926 until 1962, the year of her death.

The wound in her heart, which is 3 1/2 centimeters long x 1/2 centimeter wide.

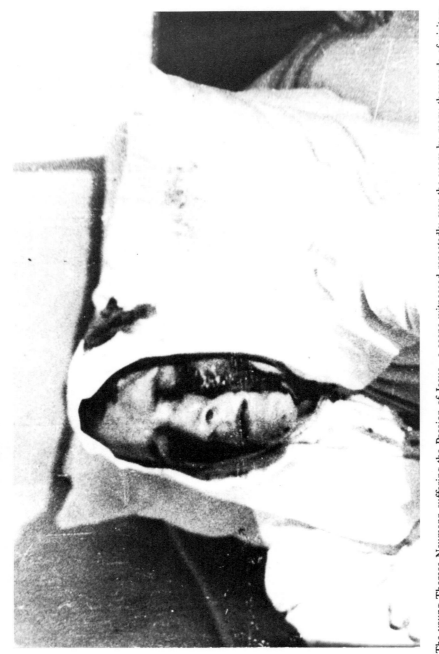

The young Therese Neumann suffering the Passion of Jesus—a scene witnessed repeatedly over the years by many thousands of visitors to the Neumann home in Konnersreuth, Germany.

CAPTIONS FOR THE COLOR PICTURES

1. The chapel at the Bavarian national shrine, Our Lady of Altötting, which Therese visited annually.

2. Pope John Paul II praying before the image of Our Lady at Altötting, the national shrine of Bavaria, on November 18, 1980. During her life Therese Neumann often had Msgr. Adalbert Vogl offer Masses in front of this holy image.

3. Miraculous reception of Holy Communion. Therese saw Our Lord, and the Host would disappear into her mouth without any swallowing.

4. Therese during a Passion ecstasy on Friday—one of approximately 725 Passion ecstasies during her life.

5. Another photograph of Therese suffering the Passion.

6. Therese's hand during a Friday Passion suffering.

7. Therese in ecstasy, seeing the saint whose feastday it is.

8a. Blood-stained night jacket of Therese, photographed in her bedroom. It is held by Fr. Salvador Jocson (a priest formerly of the San Jose diocese, now stationed in Fatima), Fr. Anton Vogl (not related to the author), Postulator of Therese's process and new pastor of Konnersreuth, and by friends of the Vogls.

8b. Blood-stained night jacket held by Albert and Esther Vogl. Note the red wall plaque containing relics of the True Cross and of St. Francis of Assisi given to Therese by Popes Pius XI and Pius XII.

9a. Blood-stained cloth held by Albert Vogl, his son Frank, and Fr. Anton Vogl, Postulator. Years ago, when Frank was a 4-year-old child visiting Germany, Therese Neumann often played with him and held him on her lap.

9b. Therese's head scarf showing 9 head wounds.

10. Bed where Therese suffered the Passion of Our Lord; on the bed are blood-stained cloths, as well as devotional articles belonging to the Vogls and others.

11a. Altar in Therese's room and cloth which covered her heart wound, showing the blood and blood clot from the wound. Cardinals and Bishops offered Mass here on numerous occasions during Therese's Passion sufferings.

11b. Birdcage in Therese's room now containing stuffed birds. During her life it was full of exotic birds given to her as gifts. When Therese suffered the Passion of Christ, the birds suffered with her; they did not eat, they acted terribly sick, and then they died with her. But soon they revived and came back to normal life.

12a. Fr. Ulrich Veh, O.F.M. Cap., one of the 2 vice postulators of Therese's process, speaking with Mr. and Mrs. Vogl and their son Frank.

12b. General view of the well-kept cemetery in Konnersreuth; Therese's grave marker is to the right of the large crucifix.

13a. The grave of Therese Neumann. The plaques in gratitude for favors received pile up constantly; when some are removed for documentation, others continue to arrive.

13b. The graves of Fr. Joseph Naber, Therese's spiritual director for over 50 years, and of other priests, including Fr. Bruno Rothschild, who was converted from Judaism through Therese.

14. & 15. The parish church of St. Lawrence in Konnersreuth; note the altar of St. Therese the Little Flower on the left. In accord with Therese Neumann's desire there are plans to move her tomb into a crypt underneath this shrine.

16. A closer view of the Shrine of St. Therese in St. Lawrence Church in Konnersreuth.

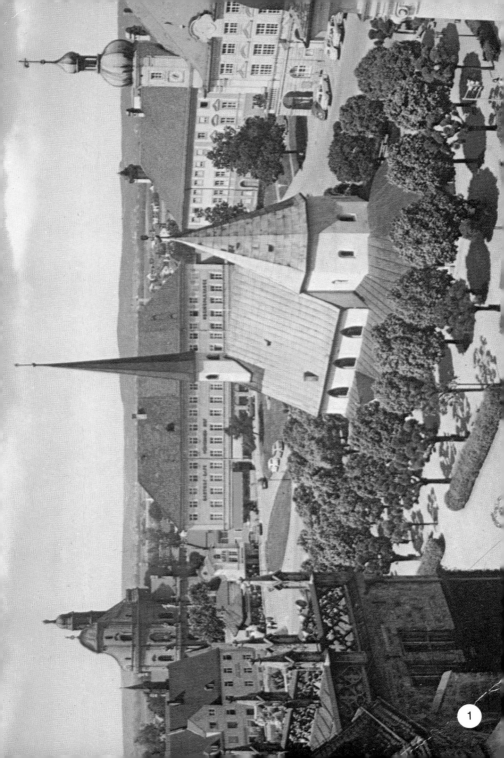

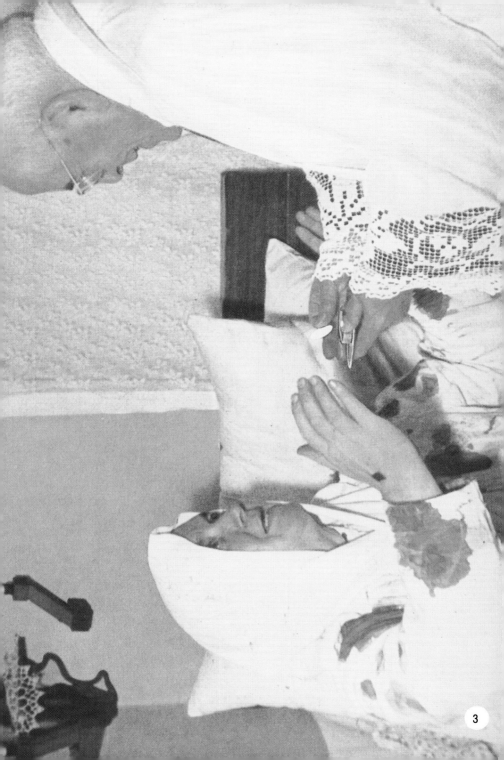

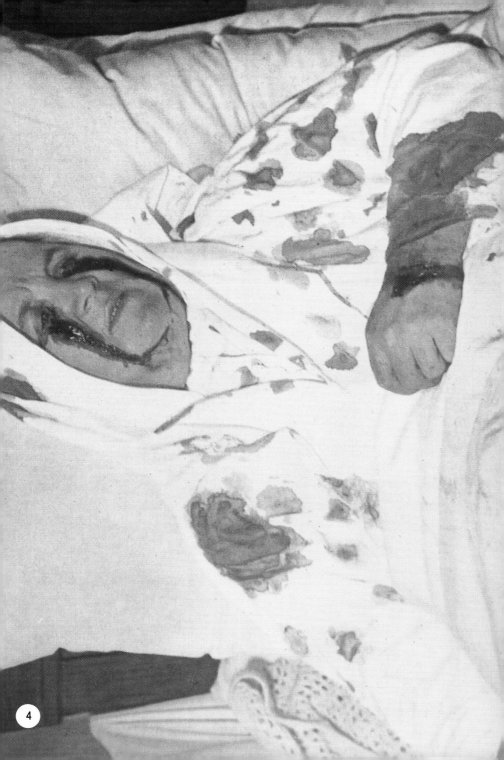

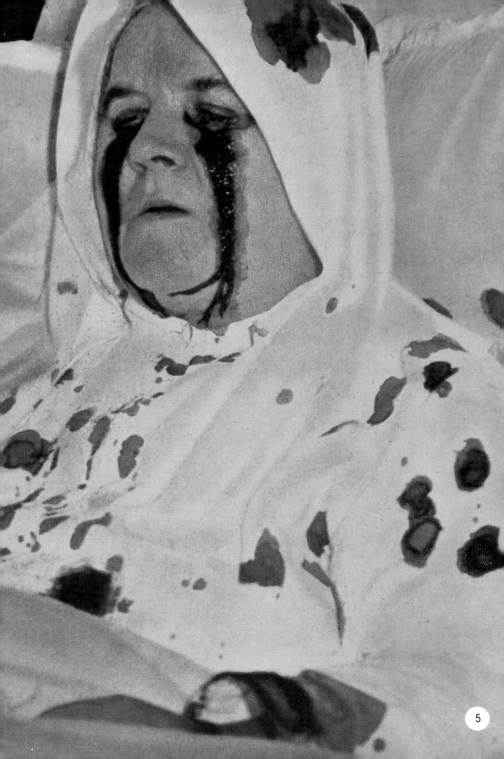

5

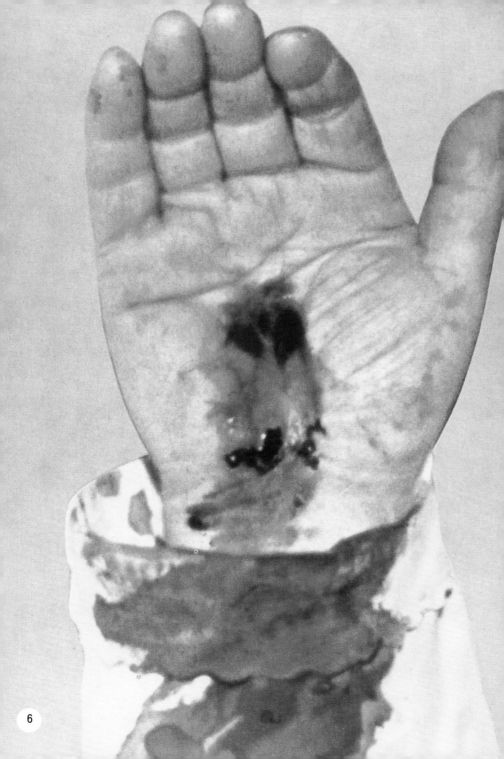

6

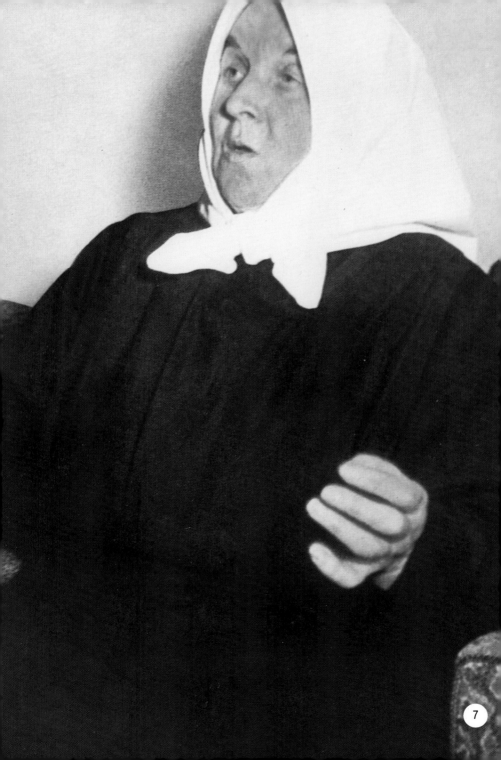

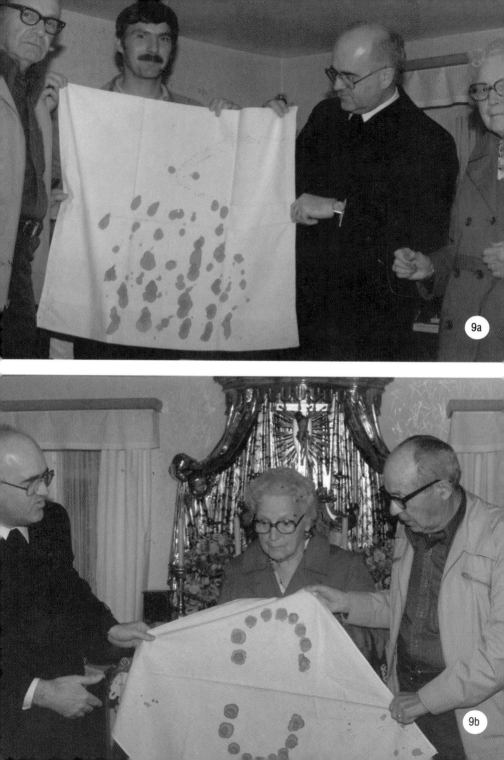

9a

9b

11a

11b

12a

12b

SCHICKER †
JOHANN 1875–1922
JOHANN 1910–1943
BERTA 1885–1965

13a

13b

PRIESTERGRÄB

MAYER JOHANN
PFARRER v. 1853–1860

RENG KARL
PFR. v. 1870–1889

PLATZER MICHAEL
PFARRER v. 1890–1890

ROTHSCHILD BR.
GEST. 24.12.1932

PFLAUM FRANZ
PFR v. hoben 15.–7.10.1935 † 3.11.1981

ICH BIN DER GUTE HIRTE UND KENNE DIE MEINEN
UND DIE MEINEN KENNEN MICH

JOSEF NABER
BISCHG. RAT 72 JAH. PRIESTER
51 JAH. PFR. i. KONNERSREUTH
44 J. SEELSORGER d. STIGMATI-
SIERTEN THERES NEUMANN
GEB. 4.12.1870 GEST. 23.2.1967

DANKE
1980

a few steps from the Neumann burial plot, and Therese personally cared for his grave during her lifetime. Later, his body was placed in a special gravesite, next to Therese's grave, as well as that of Father Naber and other priests. On All Saints' Day, November 1st, the saints of Heaven came to Therese in a vision. Bruno Rothschild was among them!

Another striking conversion resulted from Therese's ability to sense the condition of the souls of people who came to her. In 1937 a group of several women came to Konnersreuth to visit Therese. The usual crowds of people were waiting outside the rectory for a brief visit with the mystic. As their turn came, they were admitted. When they entered the room, Therese collapsed into an ecstatic condition, with very severe physical pain. Later, after everyone had left the room, it was over an hour before she returned to her normal state.

A few days later, one of the women from this group came to Father Naber and told him that she felt personally responsible for what had happened to Therese. Father Naber spoke very patiently to the woman, explaining the religious meaning of Konnersreuth to her and stressing the love of Jesus for all of us, demonstrated by His suffering and death for the sins of man. The woman told Father that although she was a Catholic, she had not been to the Sacraments for over fifty years. After her confession and the reception of Holy Communion, she expressed a joy she had not known at any time in her life, and she told Father Naber that he might describe her remarkable conversion to others. She returned to her home in New York, where she lived happily for six years until her death in 1943.

The list of converts coming out of Konnersreuth seems endless. A few of the most notable ones, in addition to Bruno Rothschild, are Dr. Fritz Gerlich, Hugo Hermann, and Paul Schondorf. Many others were convinced by what they saw in the life of Therese Neumann, and also found the True Faith in Konnersreuth.

— Chapter 15 —

THE CROWDS OF VISITORS

The keynote of Therese's life was her total commitment to the regulations and desires placed on her by Our Lord; she followed these voluntarily. Examples include her serious accident in 1918, and all the illnesses and blindness between that time and 1925, when she was miraculously cured. That period of time was the happiest period of Therese's life. She mentioned that to me once, and I have heard it from trusted friends of hers as well. Where can you find a soul holier than Therese? Any sacrifice and suffering was always a joy for her, as long as she knew it was the wish of Our Lord (*Heiland*).

With this in mind, one can understand the bitter disappointment of visitors who came from near and far, even across oceans, to Konnersreuth and were unable to see Therese Neumann. She may have had a serious period of suffering to undergo on that particular day, and, of course, that came first. Everything else had to wait. She loved people, but the large stream of people who came to see her was a heavy cross for her to carry. She always insisted that it would be better for these people to stay at home, make a visit to the Blessed Sacrament in their own church, and thus gain more graces, than to come to Konnersreuth.

One day Therese's father turned down a request for a visit by the Archbishop of Regensburg, who had come to town with a friend. On that day Therese was indisposed with mystical suffering and therefore could have no visitors, not even the Archbishop. Therese's life was ruled by God and for her there was never any compromise—not in the 20's when it began, until her dying day in 1962.

How disappointed Father Martini (professor and rector of the Sacred Heart University of Milan, who had been ordered by Pope Pius XI to do some investigating in Konnersreuth for the Vatican) and his friend must have felt when, after standing in line for hours, they finally got into the room where Therese was suffering! As they entered, they were told by the attending doctor that all visitors must leave immediately, and for the remainder of the day no more visitors would be allowed. Doctor's orders—no more and no less. Therese had a serious gall bladder problem and sometimes a breathing problem as well. On that day the pressure on the gall bladder became so bad that the physician had to act as he did.

Father Martini and his friend were naturally unhappy to be turned away, and after that it was rumored that there could be something "strange" going on in that room that needed to be investigated. They had a right to think that, but there was never any interference by any human being in Therese's life. It was God's will, first, last and always. Some of the disappointed people felt that sooner or later something would be discovered to discredit Therese—at least in part. Well, that time never came.

On several occasions I drove some 200 miles to Konnersreuth to see Therese, only to find that she was unable to have visitors on that day. I was fortunate to at least have a talk with Father Naber, or Therese's father, Ferdinand, or her brother August. Sometimes I talked to Father Naber's housekeeper, Marie Neumann, who was a sister of the mystic. After making a visit at the church (St. Lawrence), I just got into my car and drove off happily, knowing that I was at least near Therese.

No one knows for sure how many people visited Konnersreuth between the years of 1927 and 1962. The number would be in the millions. (There had been visitors even before Therese received the stigmata—though not nearly as many.) These people came from all over the world. It can be estimated that after 1945 at least half a million GIs visited Konnersreuth. The daily visitors can be numbered in the hundreds.

And on the Fridays (there were about twenty-seven during any one year when Therese experienced the Passion suffering), the visitors usually numbered from 5,000 to 7,000 people—occasionally up to 15,000. This went on for thirty-six years. Even today, busloads of people come daily—and many more on weekends.

During the Passion ecstasies, visitors lined up by twos, then were allowed to go up the stairs, through Therese's room without much stopping, and keep right on going downstairs, where many broke down in tears. The visitors had a chance to see the terrible sight for about 20 seconds; this was the only way that 7,000 people could see Therese within a few hours. High-ranking clergy and some others, however, were never under these restrictions as far as time is concerned.

In 1928-1929 a decision was reached, with the full approval of Therese and her parents, to stop—or at least slow down—the flow of people, so as not to make a pilgrimage place out of Konnersreuth. With the help of the Bishop of Regensburg, it was planned that anyone who wanted to visit Therese must have a pass from the diocesan headquarters first. I myself received a pass on two occasions. There was never any complete ban on visiting Therese.

This restricted visiting period, which did not last very long, was often misconstrued by people who were not friendly to the mystic. But just keep in mind that the Neumanns were poor people, and that as a result of wear from visitors they had had to install new flooring several times, as well as new steps leading up to Therese's room (probably seven times over the years). The original wooden steps were literally cut to pieces by over-anxious visitors and souvenir seekers. Of course, the Neumann family had to pay for all the damages. Their house, which would have lasted for decades with very little expense, was suddenly falling apart day by day. They also had to do the daily work and chores in order to make a living, poor as it was. One has to consider the hardships which these fine people went through day after day for over thirty-six years.

— *Chapter 16* —

A GREAT PRIVILEGE WAS OURS

Therese had to get permission from Our Lord to travel, and she had to make extraordinary plans for meeting people. On August 10, 1950, while I was talking to the mystic in the corridor of the parish house, just minutes after the vision of the martyrdom of St. Lawrence had ended, she said that Father Naber was working too hard, and that he should have a little rest. The thousands of visitors every week were taking too much out of him and he should have a vacation. I immediately suggested that I was ready, willing and able to help along these lines. All I had to have was "your word." I almost fainted when she took me by my elbow and said, "Mr. Vogl, would you take us to Altötting? There we could make our yearly pilgrimage to the Shrine, but we would have to be left alone." She knew my uncle and aunts there, and of course they had a nice place for her to stay. We left the conversation with the thought that she would ask permission to make the trip, and when they could go, she would write to me and give me the day of departure. I gave her a self-addressed, stamped envelope so she could give me notice of the trip. The letter which she wrote to me is shown in this book.

She then asked me if I was all alone, and I told her that my wife was waiting for me in the car, along with a nice couple we had met at the Passion Play in Oberammergau, Mr. and Mrs. Steve Andrews of Lebanon, Pennsylvania. They wanted very much to see Therese, but did not dare go to Konnersreuth on their own, for fear that they might not be able to see her. Therese told me that on this day the visiting hours were over for all people, but that we should come back the next day; we should stay at the end of the line and let

93

all the other people go into the rectory first. I agreed happily. Therese wanted to know where we would stay overnight and I mentioned that I would probably drive to Tirschenreuth and we would stay in a hotel there. She said that the vision of St. Lawrence that had just finished minutes ago took so much of her strength that she had better be left alone in meditation; she would be glad to see us on the following day. I hurried to the car to tell what had happened. The others could hardly believe their ears.

We did stay overnight in Tirschenreuth, and drove back to Konnersreuth the following afternoon at about 2:30. As we had been directed, we got in line and let the other people go ahead of us. Finally, all the people were taken care of and it would be only minutes before we got to the door.

A priest and his mother came up behind us. We had a minute or so to get acquainted. They were from St. Paul, Minnesota, and he had a letter of introduction from Archbishop Murray of St. Paul. I offered that we should stay together when we got into the house, and I also told them that it would be more than the usual one or two-minute visit with the mystic.

As the last ones left the house and we entered, Therese's sister Marie immediately recognized me and motioned us to come into the living room on the left of the entrance. There were the Andrews, my wife and I, and the two from St. Paul; and suddenly we found a teen-age boy in our group. No one knew who he was or how he got there. Therese entered the room, saw the boy, and in our presence she scolded him and told him in so many words that he was a naughty boy; he was told to leave the house at once. I tried to intervene, telling Therese that we did not object to having the boy in our group for the visit. She rejected this proposal, telling us that this was about the fifth time that afternoon that he had sneaked in with a group, and that she had let him get by with it for the short minute-like visits. So he got what he deserved.

If anyone had heard the discussion between Therese and

the teen-age boy, he might have thought that she was cranky and did not like children. Such a misconception could easily have taken place, and it probably did a thousand times. However, knowing what really did happen, all six of us agreed that we would have done the same thing.

During our visit I translated the letter from the Archbishop on behalf of the priest and his mother for Therese. I had to translate all the conversations. Therese was in a very jovial mood. She had had a very quiet day as far as visions were concerned. What this three-and-a-half-hour visit meant to me, my wife and the others could not be put into words.

Upon our leaving, Therese told me that Father Naber was delighted with the idea of a trip, and they would set a convenient time later. She said she would use the envelope I had given her and would write to me later on as to when I should take them to Altötting.

After I received the letter from Therese, my wife and I took her, Father Naber, a nephew and a niece to the city of Altötting, in the last week of September, 1950. In many ways this little journey was the most memorable experience of my life. We arrived at the home of my uncle, Father Sebastian Vogl (a university professor), and made plans for the sightseeing and the visit to the Shrine of the Mother of God. I was put in complete charge of keeping Therese's visit as free from crowds as possible, as she did not want to be recognized. Therese decided it would be best for Father Naber and the children to make their visits on their own at a different time, and she would go with me at her side. With all the pilgrims at the Shrine daily, it could become like a mob scene, and this must not happen. I also made a plan to take Therese around town by car.

The Holy Shrine was visited on the very first day, the minute we arrived in Altötting, even before we went to my uncle's home. Therese told me to park the car in an inconspicuous place and that I should go with her to the Shrine. No one recognized us, and we just acted like ordinary pilgrims. One thing helped me. As it was past nine in the evening and already dark, the shrine was filled only with pilgrims from out of town, people who would not recognize Therese. We stayed about ten minutes, and Therese took me by my hand when she was ready to leave. It made her very happy to have made the yearly visit, and her face was just beaming with joy.

The following day we went to old St. Michael's Cemetery, a most interesting 800-year-old holy place. My father and uncles were buried there, and Therese wanted to see the graves. I would not venture to say how many short visions she had in that cemetery, not only at my uncles' graves, but at others as well. I was on a time schedule, and it had to be like clockwork if we were to get to all the interesting places she wanted to visit. I had an awful time getting her out of that cemetery. When I finally did so, after repeated urging, she said, "For me it is the nicest place under the sun." Therese just loved cemeteries. I shall never forget the fifteen minutes she spent there with me. We also went to the Basilica and to the monastery where St. Conrad of Parzham had lived and died in the 19th century.

The crowd that we feared so much came on the following day, when I took her to the Schatzkammer Museum. I had called the curator and asked him to do me a favor and take me, my wife, my mother and a friend through the museum. I had known him as a child and there was no way he could refuse me. I told him that it absolutely had to be a private showing, and he agreed that it would be.

Therese was full of excitement over seeing the museum for the first time in her life. All went beautifully; the four of us enjoyed the narration about all the precious items. This lasted for a mere twenty minutes when, all of a sudden, another employee came into the museum, bringing another group for a showing. I recognized many people from Altötting, and to my great surprise, a member of the press was also present.

Somehow, somewhere we had been recognized. Therese stayed in the museum for another fifteen minutes, but we had to push our way through the crowd, which got bigger and bigger. There was nothing for me to do but to comply with Therese's wish to get her out of there as fast as possible. When we were again in the car, Therese put her head down on the back seat so she would not be seen. With much difficulty we finally made it out of the parking lot, and by way of a detour we arrived at my uncle's home. There a crowd had gathered, hoping to get a glimpse of the mystic. This ended our stay in Altötting. Therese and Father Naber agreed that their purpose had been fulfilled, and there was no way it could have been avoided.

The four of us, Therese, Father Naber, my wife and I hurriedly packed our bags and drove to Munich, where Therese wanted to have a visit with Dr. J. Mittendorfer (M.D.). Therese was with my wife in the back seat, and Father Naber sat up in front with me. What an unforgettable day that was for me! I regret that it was utterly impossible to keep the pilgrimage as private as they had wished it to be.

After a most enjoyable visit with the good doctor (the details are related elsewhere in this book), we drove on to Eichstätt, where we had a most cordial time with Therese's sister Ottilie, who lived in the home of the late Father Wutz, who had been a professor of the Old Testament and Oriental languages at the seminary in Eichstätt before his death. He had been a great help in translating Therese's words as she repeated what she heard during her ecstatic visions. Therese and her sister revered the kindly professor's memory by adorning with a beautiful shrine the spot in the garden where he had died.

We all had an especially happy and restful visit in Eichstätt with Ottilie. There were no outside interruptions, as the presence of Therese and Father Naber was kept as quiet as possible. Therese, Father Naber, and Therese's niece and nephew stayed at the Wutz estate with Ottilie; my wife Esther and I stayed at a nearby hotel. Therese told us of the plans that she had in mind for the whole week. We were to come over to their place, attend Mass, eat there, and then every day enjoy the beautiful countryside for the rest of the week. That was her wish.

Each morning we were privileged to attend Holy Mass in

the private chapel of the residence. The chapel consisted of a very beautiful altar and one large kneeling bench. Father Naber offered the Mass, and no one but Therese, her sister, a niece, a nephew, my wife and I attended—although one morning, Prince Waldburg zu Zeil, a longtime friend of Father Naber and Therese, was also present.

It was an unforgettable experience to receive Holy Communion during the Mass. As we received, the paten was passed from one to the other. My wife, kneeling next to Therese, turned to hand it to her, but she saw that Therese was already in ecstasy. The Sacred Host disappeared in Therese's mouth without any movement of swallowing.

I approached Therese and asked her for permission to make a souvenir of our first private Mass with her. Without hesitation she answered, "Why not." She walked quickly into her study room and came back, handing me a rather large picture of the Risen Christ. She said, "Take this, Mr. Vogl, there is enough room on the back for your text. We shall all write on it." The text reads as follows: In remembrance of September 21, 1950, on which day we attended Mass celebrated by Father Naber in the house chapel in Eichstätt. On that day we have also received Holy Communion in the presence of Therese Neumann.

Naber, Pastor	Ottilie Neumann
Benedikta Härtl	Konrad Härtl
Therese Neumann	Esther Vogl
Albert Vogl	

Each morning after Mass, we ate breakfast with Father Naber, while Therese helped wait on the table. Therese displayed great skill as a cook and assistant hostess. We especially recall the way that she mixed butter with the honey to enable us to spread it on our bread more easily. Father jokingly asked Therese if she were hungry. She replied that she was quite satisfied to "eat only with her eyes."

With Eichstätt as our daily starting point, we made several

trips into the surrounding countryside. One of these journeys was to a nursery where Therese and Father Naber bought some shrubbery for the Konnersreuth cemetery. I was amazed at Therese's stamina in walking through the nursery grounds for over an hour, and also at her knowledge of plant life. She knew many of the shrubs and trees by their Latin names.

While traveling, and at mealtime, my wife and I had an excellent opportunity to learn more and more about Therese's experiences and ecstasies. We received most satisfying and enlightening answers to all our questions, some of which must have taxed Father Naber's patience because of the detail we sought. The same patient response was given to every reasonable question from every interested and sincere inquirer. Nothing was for sale at Konnersreuth, nor did the slightest spirit of controversy prevail there. The one commodity which visitors could find there was a true and objective portrait of the preternatural occurrences of the last decades and the furtherance of God's glory—especially through the greater knowledge of the Saviour's sufferings which has come to thousands by reason of Therese's life.

On the last day of our visit in Eichstätt, I asked Father Naber if he could give us some idea as to the date of the next Passion ecstasy that Therese would be experiencing. Removing his breviary from its case, he turned to the ecclesiastical calendar covering the coming weeks. He told us that Friday, October 13, would be the date of her next Passion suffering, and he invited us to be present. We were happy to accept his invitation, and we looked forward with eagerness to that date. He suggested that we plan to be in Konnersreuth on the evening of the 12th, that we might observe the drama of the suffering in its entirety.

In accord with this agreement, we arrived in Konnersreuth at about six o'clock on the evening of October 12. Knowing that Therese would withdraw from the company of her family and friends as the suffering of the Passion began to envelop her, we decided to visit her first, and then go to Father Naber's rectory. Arriving at the Neumann home, we had a pleasant visit with Therese's father, her brother August and August's family. Therese was in her room upstairs and it was some minutes before she joined us. We noticed immediately that her face was deeply flushed, as though she were suffering from a high fever. Sensing her condition, we excused ourselves and would have left, but she insisted that we remain. She inquired about my family, whom she had visited a short time before, and made further inquiry about where we had been since the sojourn in Eichstätt. When we had chatted for nearly an hour, Therese told us that Father Naber was expecting us for supper, but that she would have to remain at home. Anticipating that her condition the following day would not permit her to say good-bye, she wished us God's blessing and a pleasant trip on our return to America and shook our hands while saying a most cordial *Auf Wiedersehen.*

Arriving at the rectory, we were ushered into the big Bavarian kitchen that expanded into a combination living room and dining room. After having supper with Father Naber, we enjoyed a most pleasant and enlightening evening with him, which lasted several hours. Guided by my tremendous interest in all phases of Therese's life, I brought up one question after another. The answer I received to one inquiry surprised me. I asked Father if he was sure that Therese would suffer the Passion the following day. He answered with an emphatic "Yes." He told us that if Therese was to have the suffering on a Friday, it never failed that this fact was made known to him while Therese received Holy Communion on the day before, that is, on Thursday morning. At such a time, Therese was in an ecstatic vision and he, or any other priest who gave the Holy Eucharist to her, heard the voices of angels, one directing the other to inform the priest that Therese should receive Communion one hour earlier on the following day. This was indeed a wonderful heavenly proclamation to enable Therese to receive the Bread of Life at a time when she was physically able to do so. From experience, they knew that one hour later it would be impossible for her to receive, for then she would be fully enveloped in ecstasy. Father Naber said that any priest who was present during Holy Communion on Thursday before a suffering would plainly hear the instructions of the angels.

The next day, Friday, we did indeed witness Therese's Passion suffering, for about two hours, and watched that dreadful agony and bleeding and gasping. It is something we will never forget.

— *Chapter 17* —

GOOD FRIDAY OF 1951

Many people have inquired as to what happened on Good Friday of 1951. Much ado was made of the fact that Therese did not experience the Passion of Our Lord on that day. Here is what happened, just as Father Naber described it to me.

It was a cold, rainy day; nevertheless, over 10,000 visitors had come to Konnersreuth from near and far to get a glimpse of Therese. Many American soldiers were among those assembled. Then something occurred that had never happened before. At 8:15 a.m. Father Naber made an announcement over the public address system (which had been placed at his disposal by the traffic officer). He astonished the crowds with these words: "Due to circumstances beyond our control, no one will be allowed to see or visit Therese Neumann today. The suffering and the bleeding of the wounds will not take place today!"

This caused excitement, and anyone who has been in Konnersreuth on such a day can sympathize with Father Naber. After Mass he consented to the wishes of the curious crowds and made a more detailed explanation of what had happened. He told them that Our Lord had appeared to Therese earlier in the morning and said to her: "Today is the twenty-fifth Jubilee of your stigmata and of the 500th ecstasy of My Passion and death. In recognition of this double Jubilee, you will not have to suffer or bleed as you have in the past. You will, nevertheless, take part in the vision of My Passion."

Father Naber went on to explain that the Saviour had promised Therese that this would in no way mean the end of her ecstasies. He told her that there would be a resumption and continuation of all these in the future, just as in the past.

In the mild, humble manner that has always characterized Father Naber, he pleaded with the disappointed thousands to understand that divine intervention, and not Therese or anyone else, had altered what had become traditional at Konnersreuth.

Whereas the parish priest saw in the non-occurrence of Therese's physical suffering and bleeding a very special dispensation of Divine Providence, the curious and the thrill-seekers and the mockers concluded that this would bring some embarrassment to Therese and her friends. Father Naber and the Neumann family were as much surprised by the non-occurrence of Therese's suffering that day as was anyone among the crowd of visitors. The critics who had sometimes concluded that Father Naber controlled Therese's ecstasies knew that now they would have to contrive some other explanation.

It had always been the wish of the priest and of Therese that people should keep only one thing in mind when they came to Konnersreuth—not Therese's suffering, but rather the suffering which Christ Himself endured for our sins. Their wish was that people should come closer to His Sacred Heart. Therese did not want any theater-like sensation, and would doubtless have preferred to endure her sufferings in sheltered privacy. Any exploitation of Therese's experiences bringing any material advantage to anyone has remained utterly absent from the spirit of dedication to the mystery of the Passion as it was relived in Konnersreuth.

— Chapter 18 —

THE NEUMANN FAMILY

The Neumann family were humble, God-fearing people. They wanted nothing for themselves but a peaceful life in this world and salvation in the next. All this publicity was thrust upon them, and it was not easy to deal patiently with the thousands of visitors who came to their door.

There were many offers to commercialize on Therese's fame, but these honest, hard-working, humble villagers had absolutely no thought or desire to exploit the phenomena that made Therese's life so notable. Rather, they preferred to resignedly accept the will of God as it was manifest in her experiences and to cheerfully bear the sacrifices occasioned by the ogling and sometimes inconsiderate public. The loss of time alone was very costly, for their work was constantly being interrupted—yet they never accepted a cent from any visitor, regardless of how wealthy he may have been.

It is inconceivable that people of such integrity would have stooped to the "tricks" that are sometimes alleged, in order to make Therese appear to be something she was not. What would they have gained? They suffered much from slander and criticism, but it is really wonderful how they all accepted Therese's condition as the will of God, and how they cooperated in every possible way to ease her cross.

Many mystics have not been so fortunate as to have an understanding family to care for them during their sufferings. Therese was ever thankful, and enjoyed the deepest affection and loyalty of her entire family.

— Chapter 19 —

FATHER NABER

Another great blessing which Therese enjoyed was to have the same spiritual director from the very beginning of her mystical experiences. Many mystics have not been so privileged, and it was a source of anguish to them to change spiritual directors, or to have one who was not sufficiently gifted to understand and guide them.

Father Joseph Naber was the pastor in Konnersreuth from 1909 to 1960. He was the essence of kindness, which he radiated with his snow-white hair and his calm, intelligent face that smiled so readily. He had the "patience of a saint," relating over and over again to thousands of visitors the story of Therese and her sufferings. He never refused to answer a sincere and earnest question, regardless of how irrelevant or trifling it might have seemed. Although he was 97 years old when he died, Our Lord blessed him with the endurance and vitality of a much younger man.

Father Naber was loved and respected by the people of Konnersreuth. This worthy priest cared for his flock in a most serious manner. He was interested in all their daily problems, and guided them toward their eternal reward in a manner that must surely have made the One Shepherd very happy. Therese, an especially chosen one, was given much of his time and attention. He felt deeply the responsibility that God had given him to care for this special child of God. He accepted it as the will of God. His manner with Therese was gentle and fatherly, and he loved to joke with her in his droll fashion.

His implicit faith in Therese is shown in an experience I had in 1950. At that time, Father Naber had been Therese's spiritual director for forty-three years. I was asked to be an interpreter so that Father could converse with some American priests. The inevitable question arose regarding Therese's total abstinence from food since 1922. The exact words which Father Naber used to emphasize the truth of the fact were: *"Das kann ich Ihnen mit meinem Leben versichern."* (That I can assure you with my life!)

Therese had great concern for the well-being of her pastor and spiritual director. She made proper plans for a worthy home for this saintly priest by turning the Neumann home over to the parish as a retirement home for Father Naber. He retired to a new apartment next to and connected with Therese's upstairs apartment in the old Neumann house. (Father Schumann came as new pastor.) He lived there until his death in 1967. At that time, in accord with Therese's desire, the home was turned over to the Sisters of Mt. Carmel who lived in the nearby convent. (These are the same sisters as those of the cloister "Theresianum," the story of which is told in a later chapter.) Under the direction of the local parish priest, the sisters have maintained the home in a manner befitting the people who lived there and the events which occurred there.

A book by Father Naber, consisting of the reports on Therese Neumann which he made almost weekly to the bishop of Regensburg, has just recently been published (in German). It is entitled *From the Daily Diary of the Life of Therese Neumann* (and it bears an Imprimatur from the Archdiocese of Munich). Father Naber had to deal with Bishops Antonius Henle, Michael Buchberger and Rudolf Gräber, and his testimony is of the highest value in the case of Therese Neumann.

— *Chapter 20* —

A SEMINARY FOR LATE VOCATIONS

Therese Neumann told me in late fall of 1950, during our week-long vacation trip (see Chapter 15), that when we arrived in Eichstätt we would meet Prince Waldburg zu Zeil. She told me that he owned a large estate in Württemberg, and that he had lost much lumber and other valuables to the army of occupation (the Allied armies had cut down a large section of his forests), although this was in violation of the Peace Treaty. I was told that if the prince could get this tremendous loss refunded to him by the occupation forces, he would turn over a large share of the money to Therese. At that time her plan was already set to do everything humanly possible to procure a certain estate a couple of miles outside Konnersreuth. This property used to be called Fockenfeld, but during the anti-Catholic period in Germany called "Sekularization," it had been taken from the Church and put into private hands.

This estate dates back to the year 1311. In the state title register it is classified as an estate called "Vokkenvelle." At the end of the 14th century, this property was incorporated into that of the famous monastery of nearby Waldsassen. In 1750 it was used as a summer home for the abbots of the Waldsassen monastery. However, as mentioned above, the Catholic Church lost this, and so many other Church properties, through the secularization in 1803. (I have always said that Bismarck stole the Catholic Church blind, and that Hitler wanted to *kill* the Church.) The property of Fockenfeld was kicked around, so to speak, and it passed through numerous different hands—ten, to be exact. Of course, it ended up in the hands of non-Catholics.

Then along came Therese Neumann; the time was 1950 and 1951. It so happened that a Dr. Mittendorfer, who was an advisor of Therese regarding her medical condition, was also treating the owner of the estate of which we are now talking. Dr. Mittendorfer had a certain amount of influence on his patient regarding the eventual sale of this beautiful property. Therese had had her eye on it, and had made known that she wanted it in order to establish a seminary for late vocations (men entering the seminary after the usual age). But there was so much money involved that the idea seemed to die away.

Finally, Therese's prayers and sacrifices were answered when Prince Waldburg zu Zeil became a good friend of hers, as well as a friend of Father Naber and the Neumann family. The opportunity to help this man receive compensation for the loss of his property was an opportunity which Therese used for the glory of Our Lord. She wanted enough money to buy Fockenfeld—not for herself or her family, but to convert it into a seminary for late priestly and religious vocations and to improve the agricultural land contained in the parcel.

Thousands of U.S. Army personnel visited Konnersreuth every week from 1945 until Therese's death in 1962. On many occasions Therese met high-ranking officers. This gave her an opportunity to discuss her plan for the purchase of Fockenfeld for this worthy cause. Through the help of visitors in Konnersreuth, Therese became acquainted with a Mr. Werner, who was stationed in Frankfurt. He was a high official of the United States connected with war reparations. Therese was driven to Frankfurt to see Mr. Werner, and eventually the case was cleared in court in favor of Prince Waldburg zu Zeil. This noble friend kept his word and loaned enough money (at a very special low interest rate) to the Oblate Fathers of St. Francis de Sales in Eichstätt, who were thus able to buy the property of Fockenfeld in 1951.

Today Fockenfeld is a seminary for late vocations, with beautiful cultivated land surrounding it. It is run by the Oblate Fathers of St. Francis de Sales, having been blessed and put into operation by Archbishop Michael Buchberger of Regensburg on October 3, 1955.

It was only through Therese's missionary zeal and love for Our Lord that such a tremendous plan could have been brought to a satisfactory conclusion. All this was for the glory of God, through the worthy servant, Therese Neumann. No one in Konnersreuth or Regensburg will deny the fact that without Therese's help this would never have been accomplished.

At the last communication I had with a priest from Fockenfeld, the seminary was doing very well, with twenty-five men studying for the priesthood. I am informed by Father Anton Vogl that many priests and brothers have graduated from Fockenfeld and have been ordained or have taken their vows. As of Autumn, 1986 there have been over 250 priestly ordinations. Priests who are ordained there go not only to the diocese of Regensburg but to places all over Bavaria and Germany. In my estimation this is an extraordinary accomplishment, particularly in our materialistic times.

— Chapter 21 —

THE LAST PROJECT AND DEATH
OF THERESE NEUMANN

A short time after Dr. Rudolf Gräber was made Bishop of Regensburg, he wrote a letter to Therese Neumann asking her to pray and offer up sacrifices for a very worthy cause which was close to his heart. (He had been a longtime devoted friend of Therese Neumann from the days when he was Bishop of Eichstätt; he came to Konnersreuth quite frequently.) The Bishop told Therese that he would be most happy to have a convent for Perpetual Adoration in the diocese.

Therese was delighted to accept this request, as she loved challenges for the cause of Our Lord. She prayed, and suffered, and planned, and used all her influence with so many prominent people, as well as with the broad masses of common folk. Soon this request of her Bishop started to blossom into great enthusiasm. Her zeal to work for this worthy project was utmost in her mind in her daily activities. The Bishop had pointed out in his letter that such a convent should be used primarily to pray for the intentions of the Bishop and also for the needs of the diocese.

It so happened that a short time after the request, a plot of ground on the outskirts of Konnersreuth was offered to Therese for her personal intentions. It fell right into her plan. She now knew that this was the place for the erection of the convent. The Bishop was quick to give his approval of the location. With her intuitive knowledge, Therese was foremost in planning and getting things accomplished. Just remember that years earlier she had single-handedly done the very same thing regarding the purchase of a large estate and the building of a seminary for late vocations. That experience no doubt helped her, and the plans for the new convent moved ahead rapidly.

In her wonderful way of planning, Therese Neumann also called upon her wonderful friend in Heaven, St. Therese, who was a Carmelite. She thought, "Would it not be appropriate to have a Carmelite convent in Konnersreuth?" Immediately she got the wheels turning, and with the help of the Bishop they approached the Carmelites of Regensburg (also called Sisters of Mary of Mt. Carmel, or Marian Sisters of Mt. Carmel). The plan worked. The Superior was delighted with the idea and promised Therese that she would transfer at least five sisters to the new convent in Konnersreuth at the outset.

With a number of co-workers—and there were many enthusiastic helpers—Therese collected furniture, plumbing and everything necessary to begin operating the new convent.

Therese worked feverishly on this project, even though there was always so much to do during her daily routine. As an example, between the years 1952 and 1962 alone, she wrote over 1,500 letters. I have talked to people who saw the list of addresses all properly recorded. In spite of the pain that writing caused her hand wounds, she did all this for the love of God and her fellow men.

Toward the end of August, 1962, the plans were so far advanced that it was time to make a trip to Württemberg to see a good friend who was a generous donor for the cause of Konnersreuth. Therese decided on this trip with Father Naber, endless worker in the vineyard of Christ even at his age of 92. They drove first to Eichstätt to visit some good friends there, and then they started the long trip to the southwestern part of Germany. At the residence of a famous family she met the Bishop of Fatima and Cardinal Bea, S.J., of the Roman Curia. This family, Count Georg and Countess Monika-Waldburg-Zeil, were longtime friends of Therese, and no request to help her in her undertakings was ever turned down.

Keep in mind that Therese had a serious heart problem. As a matter of fact, she had a mild attack shortly before they left Bavaria. I never saw a person in all my life with the zeal she had for the cause of Our Lord. This went on day and night.

I can well imagine the long meetings they must have had in Weingarten, southern Germany, to iron out all the various details for the final construction of the new convent. Before Therese left, the Bishop of Fatima, knowing that Therese loved birds so much, gave her a beautiful white dove. How happy she must have been! I can very well imagine, for I remember the time I drove her to Marktredwitz on the 15th of October, 1953 and went shopping with her. The first place she stopped was a pet shop, and I bought a bird for her. She was like a child in her delight.

The final transaction for the convent project came to a successful conclusion, and on the 9th of September Therese and Father Naber returned to Bavaria. It was a most happy homecoming, so much had been accomplished. Friends shared Therese's delight over the progress that had been made, and also over the lovely gift from the Bishop of Fatima. Therese and Father Naber were overjoyed with their visit with the Bishop and Cardinal Bea, and with the generosity of their good friends the Count and Countess.

Therese's condition suddenly began to deteriorate. It almost seemed as if her work on earth was done. The contracts for the new convent were secured and the word was "Go ahead." As a daily communicant, Therese was resigned to anything that might come.

Father Naber celebrated Holy Mass for her in their private chapel (he was of course retired), and he saw that Therese's condition was not getting any better. He became greatly concerned. After Holy Communion one day while she was in the "exalted rest" period, during which she could always see things way ahead, he asked her as her spiritual director how this would end if her health did not improve. She answered, "The decision will come next Tuesday."

It turned out that the following Tuesday was the last time she could receive Our Lord in Holy Communion. It was a miraculous Communion, an event which usually happened only on high feastdays; the Host appeared on Therese's tongue, having been given her by Our Lord Himself. The time was 10:30 a.m.

After the vision and the reception of Our Lord, Therese was fully conscious, and during an attack she was still able to ring for her sister Marie. Therese appeared to be very uncomfortable, and it was apparent that the death struggle was in progress. Marie was greatly alarmed and immediately called Father Naber. As he stepped into the room, Therese Neumann had already presented her holy soul to her dear Lord and Saviour Jesus Christ. Thus on September 18, 1962, one of the greatest mystics and stigmatists of our time passed to her eternal reward.

Father Schumann, the pastor of Konnersreuth, pronounced the ritual of the Catholic Church and administered the Last Sacraments. No one in the room really believed that Therese was dead. She had died more than a hundred deaths in her lifetime, and many times everyone thought of her permanent passing from this earth. Candles were often lit on such occasions, because there was no pulse, no breathing or heartbeat; and she had often been pronounced dead by doctors. However, this time, after a period of hours had passed, they finally called in three doctors, who eventually pronounced her dead.

Like wildfire the news went around Europe and the world. Wisely, the doctors were ordered to watch and check the body of Therese, starting Tuesday, September 18 until the following Saturday before the coffin was closed for the funeral. The scientific verdict after the final examination by the doctors was: there existed no death odor, no death spots, and there was no death stiffness. Also, there was no breathing, and Therese's lips remained fresh and moist.

It must be remembered that in Germany no one is embalmed, as people are in the U.S.A. Furthermore, the record shows that at the time of Therese's death on Tuesday until the funeral on Saturday, Konnersreuth was suffering from a heat wave. Still, there were no signs of death, as would ordinarily be true. Before the coffin was closed on Saturday, the doctors made a final check of the inside of Therese's body and intestines for historical purposes. They inserted a long instrument and pierced her internal organs. There was no sign of decay, no sign of death, and the blood and tissues were as normal as in any living human being. These facts are now a matter of record.

Therese Neumann's funeral was the largest that had ever occurred in Konnersreuth. Letters and telegrams were sent to the family and to the parish from all over the world. Bishops, high Church dignitaries, statesmen and over 10,000 people attended the beautiful ceremonies of the Christian burial of Therese Neumann. The eulogies of prominent high-ranking officials of Church and state were indeed beautiful and dignified.

As a postscript to the passing of our dear Therese, I would like to mention some of the last ecstasies she had. These were: the Exaltation of the Holy Cross on September 14, 1962, the Seven Dolors of the Blessed Virgin Mary on September 15, and finally, the visions of the stigmatization of St. Francis of Assisi on September 17. Cardinal Bea, S.M. was her last most notable visitor from the Vatican shortly before she died. He asked for her prayers for the Ecumenical Council. After Therese was buried on September 22, the Bishop of Fatima offered up Holy Mass at the altar in her bedroom, the room where she had died. Among the thousands of visitors at the graveside of Therese was the Apostolic Nuncio to West Germany, Archbishop Corrado Bafile.

Therese had completed the legalities for the building of the Carmelite convent. Without any loss of time, this plan was put into effect right after her death. Within months the parish celebrated the groundbreaking ceremonies. The Bishop of Regensburg, Rudolf Gräber, and other Church dignitaries performed the services and the blessing of the ground. For this monumental ceremony people came from all over

Germany, and even from overseas.

The official estimate of the number of people present in Konnersreuth on that day, in that little town where Therese had been born and where she had lived all her life, was 50,000—and it is doubly gratifying for the friends of the mystic to know that seven Catholic Bishops came to celebrate with the masses of people the great joy of the work and desires of Therese Neumann. The Bishop announced in his dedication speech that the convent would be called "Theresianum" in honor of St. Therese—and, of course, the local Therese. In his sermon the Bishop pointed out in a beautiful way how the grain of wheat is planted in the ground, where it dies—only to be resurrected to bear fruit. The Bishop's talk was most edifying and made reference to the wonderful life Therese had lived while on earth. Thus the Bishop commemorated in a very special way the death of Therese Neumann.

Since 1963 the Carmelite sisters' convent of Perpetual Adoration has been in full operation; it is a spiritual haven in Konnersreuth for the thousands of visitors. (Between January and August of 1986, 150 large packed buses arrived at the convent.) It can truly be said that the Theresianum is the pride of the diocese—and the same can also be said of "Fockenfeld," the seminary for late vocations, which was Therese's earlier accomplishment.

— Chapter 22 —

THE DEATHS OF PERSONS CLOSE TO
THERESE NEUMANN

The story of the conversion of Bruno Rothschild of Vienna is recounted earlier in this writing (Chapter 13). However, there is need for further clarification regarding his death. Later investigations necessitate that I do this.

Bruno Rothschild was a young druggist. After becoming friendly with Therese, as well as with Father Naber and the Neumann family, he was baptized by Father Naber in Konnersreuth. Shortly thereafter, he decided to study for the priesthood. Through the kind help and spiritual guidance of Father Wutz of Eichstätt, Bruno had no problem being accepted. He was ordained a priest by the Bishop of Eichstätt in the summer of 1932. On Christmas of the same year he received an invitation from the Neumann family to spend the holiday in Konnersreuth.

Bruno was disinherited by his Jewish family in Vienna; thus, Konnersreuth and Eichstätt became his second home. He was immensely happy with the new environment, and the future for him in the service of God looked very bright indeed. Following the invitation for Christmas, he set out for his destination by train on Christmas Eve. In the Nuremberg central railroad station he suddenly became ill, and died of a serious heart attack.

Before word was received in Konnersreuth of the sad news, Therese had her beautiful annual vision of the birth of Christ. To her astonishment, during the ecstatic vision she saw Father Bruno Rothschild beside the Christ Child. Upon completion of the ecstasy, as was always the case after her mystical experiences, Therese could tell Father Naber or anyone what she had seen. The joy and the sadness were indeed great in Konnersreuth. Some hours later, news was received of the happenings in Nuremberg.

At Therese's request, Father Rothschild's body was transferred to Konnersreuth. He was buried in the cemetery near the Neumann plot, but was later transferred to a new plot that was reserved for the priests of Konnersreuth and, next to it, the Neumann family. Therese saw to it personally, while alive, serving the grave in a most dignified manner. The death of Father Bruno Rothschild made Therese happy for several obvious reasons, one being that with the Nazi persecution of Jews or former Jews, he might have been sent to one of the notorious concentration camps. Instead, Father Bruno was in Heaven.

The name of Father Wutz, a Ph.D. and eminent professor, appears several times in my writing. As pointed out so correctly, he and Prof. Dr. Wessely of Vienna were the main consultants for the evaluation of the numerous manifestations and assertions of Therese regarding the various dialects spoken in the Holy Land at the time of Christ. Therese's accounts of the dominant customs in those days had to be evaluated for their correctness in the finest detail. Both of these men were regarded in European intellectual circles as being the most qualified to do this work. They agreed that Therese Neumann, with her seventh-grade education, knew more about the languages and customs of those times than any known expert in the field.

Father Wutz had suffered from a heart condition beginning in 1936. On St. Joseph's Day in 1938, as he was enjoying a moment of relaxation in his garden in Eichstätt, he had a fatal heart attack. His death came very unexpectedly and was a terrible shock to Therese. She mentioned to trusted friends afterwards that Father Wutz had been allowed by Our Lord to suffer his short stay in Purgatory right there within the chapel of his home in Eichstätt. The Nazi Gestapo had been ruthlessly after him, and his death prevented inevitable arrest by Hitler.

Therese's sister Ottilie was a saintly, hard-working house-keeper for Father Wutz for over thirty-five years. She died in Eichstätt on Friday, May 1, 1959, the Feast of the Sacred Heart of Jesus. Before Ottilie died, Therese, who was present, fell into ecstasy and had a beautiful vision of the guardian angel of their deceased brother, Engelbert, who had died at the age of forty-five in 1949; of the guardian angel of their mother; and of the guardian angel of a little sister. The guardian angel of Ottilie herself came down from Heaven to lift up Ottilie and disappear in a white cloud.

Then, suddenly, the Saviour appeared. Therese saw Ottilie very plainly and witnessed the disappearance of Christ in a beautiful light. Then their father, Ferdinand Neumann, also appeared to Therese in a vision. She immediately motioned: "Why don't they take him along, too?" The father, who had died the same year, was still in Purgatory, though for a short while; later in the year, on All Saints' Day, Therese saw her own dad in Heaven.

Another convert of Konnersreuth, Paul Lütten, decided to study theology in Eichstätt and was ordained a priest there in 1940. Paul was formerly a dance instructor. He came to Konnersreuth, saw Therese several times, changed his life around totally, and worked in the vineyard of the Lord. Earlier, I mentioned the celebration of his first Holy Mass in the Cathedral in Eichstätt. On the return home from this Mass, on a very hot July day, Therese Neumann suffered a sun stroke and half of her body was paralyzed. This condition was cured on the Feast of the Assumption, August 15, 1940. While stationed in Munich, Father Paul died in a streetcar accident in 1946.

Therese's mother died on September 12, 1949; her dad on November 26, 1959; her sister Marie (housekeeper for Father Naber) on June 13, 1963; and Father Naber died at the age of 97 on the 23rd of February, 1967. He was buried in a special plot reserved for priests in the cemetery of Konnersreuth. He lies near the grave of Bruno Rothschild, Therese Neumann and the entire Neumann family. He was, without any doubt, the most revered priest of the diocese. Certainly he was the oldest active priest, the most illustrious and the best known. He was the spiritual director and pastor of St. Lawrence parish in Konnersreuth for over fifty years. Some years before Therese died, she made arrangements so that Father Naber would have a comfortable home for the rest of his life. For that purpose she was influential in getting the Neumann home turned over to the Carmelite Sisters; there quarters were reserved for the aged Father Naber. That is where he died. At present the Carmelite Sisters live there and preserve Therese's home as a memorable sanctuary.

Dr. Fritz Gerlich was one of the most courageous men of Germany who fought with all his might, intellect, and influence to stem the tide of Hitler's heathen and revolutionary National Socialism, as well as the eventual destruction of the homeland—and also the eventual persecution of Christians and Jews. In his early youth, Dr. Gerlich was a member of a Calvinist sect, but was reputedly very uninterested in his religion. He became one of Germany's foremost newspaper editors and was regarded as one of the most qualified experts in that field.

Dr. Gerlich became editor of southern Germany's largest newspaper, the *Münchener Neueste Nachrichten*. In that position, he became acquainted with the extraordinary occurrences of Konnersreuth. As a skeptic and ridiculer of anything supernatural, he was urged, and received permission, to cover the case in Konnersreuth personally. After many trips there for that purpose, he became a close friend of Therese and Father Naber, as well as of the Neumann family. Nothing could stop him from investigating all aspects of the unusual life of the now-famous Therese in those important years of 1926 and 1927. Dr. Gerlich and his wife were converted to the Catholic faith in 1928.

The conversion was handled by a very prominent missionary, theologian, and great apostle of the Bavarian Youth Organization, Father Ingbert Naab, O.F.M. Cap., of the Catholic Seminary of Eichstätt, Bavaria. On the Feast of St. Michael in 1931, both Dr. and Mrs. Gerlich received Holy Communion in the Benedictine Convent of St. Walburg, outside Eichstätt.

With great pride, Therese Neumann showed me a photo taken on that memorable day. Pictured were some of the most influential men and leaders of Catholic life in that part of Bavaria, such as Rev. Father Cosmas, O.F.M. Cap.; Father Joseph Naber of Konnersreuth; Father Wutz of Eichstätt; Count Waldburg zu Zeil; Dr. Med. Weimann; Father Lechner, theologian from Eichstätt; the Abbess of the Benedictine Convent, Sister M. Benedikta von Spiegel, a lifelong personal friend of Therese Neumann; and, of course, Therese was also present, along with Father Ingbert Naab. A short time later the new converts received the Sacrament of Confirmation from Cardinal Michael von Faulhaber of Munich.

After Hitler came to power, the tremendous fight against the Catholic Church became intensified as the months went by. Even then, Dr. Gerlich drove to Stuttgart to see the then Prime Minister of Württemberg, Dr. Bolz, trying to influence him to ease the anti-religious laws and lessen the tension that was becoming more and more a handicap between the Church and State.

On his return to Munich, Dr. Gerlich was told by a trusted informer that his office would be stormed by the Gestapo. He asked for protection from the police but was told that he was going only on hearsay, and that there was nothing to the report of any storming. Friends of Dr. Gerlich advised him in earnest to get into his car and flee to Switzerland. Dr. Gerlich rejected this and told his co-patriots that he would fight with them for the cause of the homeland and the Church. He would not become a weakling when he was needed so badly in the upcoming struggle for truth and justice.

It is of great importance to know that after his conversion to Catholicism, Dr. Gerlich relinquished the high position he had held with the secular newspaper. With the help of Catholic intellectuals, he started a new paper called *Der Gerade Weg* (*The Straight Path*). In it, for months Dr. Gerlich unmasked the policies of the Third Reich so that people would know what to expect if the trend of socialism under Hitler was not stopped. This, of course, infuriated the Hitler government.

All the opponents of Hitler's regime were put on a blacklist for persecution. On an evening in the second week in March, 1933, Gerlich's offices were indeed stormed by a contingent of Storm Troopers. The end result of this action was the utter destruction of Dr. Gerlich's offices and printing equipment, while he and all his co-workers were beaten half to death with clubs; they were kicked and hit with rifle butts.

It is a fact that during the interview of these prisoners in the Hitler headquarters later that evening, Himmler and Heydrich were present. Gerlich was separated from the others and taken to the concentration camp in Dachau where, daily, he was beaten cruelly, according to witnesses. During the night of June 30 to July 1st, 1934 he was finally beaten to death.

Dr. Fritz Gerlich will go down in history as one of the most courageous fighters in the cause of truth and justice in a free society, and also as an apostle of Christ and His Church. That he was one of the greatest intellectual backers of Therese Neumann is a well-known fact. As a legacy he left us a most eloquent, scientific, beautiful literary work— two famous volumes on Therese Neumann of Konnersreuth.

It is significant that this noble man played a very important part in the knowledge I personally received regarding Therese Neumann. My uncle, Msgr. Karl Vogl, a very prominent Catholic newspaper editor, became acquainted with Dr. Gerlich in about 1927. Uncle Karl was one of the men who influenced Gerlich to go to Konnersreuth and see for himself. Dr. Gerlich visited my uncles in Altötting many times. They became good friends and constantly exchanged views on the developments in Konnersreuth. With pride I look over documents from the early days of Therese. One of these documents was written by Dr. Gerlich to my Uncle Karl in Altötting. I quote: "In high esteem to my spiritual clerical friend, Msgr. Karl Vogl." This document was saved from the estate of my uncle.

Most of the other papers were destroyed during the many house searches which the Gestapo conducted at my uncles' homes.

My Uncle Karl lost his right to publish his paper (*Altöttinger Liebfrauenbote*) the day after Hitler came to power, and was put into involuntary retirement and watched closely under the eyes of the Gestapo. Harassed by the Gestapo day and night, he finally died a natural death in 1938. Uncle Adalbert, as I have written earlier, was publicly executed by the Gestapo along with five other prominent citizens just twenty-four hours before the army of liberation entered Altötting in April of 1945. It is true that these two martyrs, who have long enjoyed eternal happiness, were responsible for my getting acquainted with Therese Neumann. I shall ever be grateful for their generosity.

One other priest who stood out most prominently in the life of Therese Neumann was Father Ingbert Naab, O.F.M. Cap., a very holy priest previously mentioned as the one who received Dr. and Mrs. Gerlich into the Church. From 1929 to 1932 he was superior of the famous Capuchin monastery of Eichstätt, as also a prominent theologian, missionary, editor and youth leader. Besides carrying out his priestly functions he was, along with Father Naber, a highly qualified backer who spent much time in Konnersreuth with the mystic. And when Therese was in Eichstätt, he was there whenever possible, at Father Wutz's residence, where Therese spent so much time.

These two prominent churchmen, as well as Fathers Lechner and F. X. Mayer, both professors of theology, were lifelong friends of Therese and her most ardent backers in all phases of her mystical and stigmatic life. Father Naab, like all the other priests mentioned, was under strict Gestapo surveillance under the Hitler regime. Further, in 1932 Father Naab had courageously published an "Open Letter to Hitler" (reproduced here in an Appendix) in which he clearly pointed out to this lapsed Catholic his grievous wrongdoings and exhorted him to examine his conscience before God and to admit his guilt. Twenty million copies of this letter were printed; it was printed in the newspaper *Der Gerade Weg* of March 20, 1932. For this reason Father Naab had an additional reason to fear the Gestapo.

Father Naab was warned one day by a trusted friend that his name had been put on the death list of the Gestapo. This meant that any agent could kill him, with no questions asked. That evening he shaved his long Capuchin beard. Friends dressed him in ordinary salesman's clothing and whisked him off secretly to the Swiss border, where Catholic informers helped him across to safety. There he labored for the Church under an assumed name, Peter Peregrinus. As such he managed to work as a missionary in the Sudetanland (in northern Czechoslovakia), until there also the trail of persecution became too hot. He finally managed, via Switzerland, to move to Strassburg in France. As a stateless person he suffered greatly, to the point of a nervous collapse. Strassburg became the last city of his priestly activities; he died there in 1935.

During my visit to Bavaria in 1975 and while interrogating dozens of most reliable people who were longtime friends of Therese, I was able to have the case of Father Naab further verified and evaluated. It is absolutely true that Therese foretold the Gestapo surveillance of his person and that the day would be set by the Gestapo to arrest him and place him in a concentration camp. But she also mentioned, years before this happened, that he would be rescued in time, that he would be able to flee to a foreign country with a false passport, and that he would die in the monastery where he had entered the Capuchin order. The friends of Therese, at least at that time, thought this very unlikely, because Father Ingbert Naab had entered the Order in Königshofen near Strassburg in France. But as time proved, every little detail came through just as foretold by Therese.

After the war was ended, the people of Eichstätt expressed the desire to transfer the body of their beloved Father Naab back to Eichstätt, which he always loved and considered his home. The Lord Mayor of Eichstätt, Dr. Hutter, had this accomplished in 1953. There in the mausoleum of the Capuchin monastery Father Naab's body rests, awaiting the final Resurrection.

It seems to me that there is a dramatic comparison between the persecution by the forces of evil as suffered by the Apostles of Christ and as suffered by the holy men who were Therese Neumann's friends, advisors, backers, and ardent believers. Several other fine priests, as well as lay people, would no doubt have spent their last hours in concentration camps had it not been for their early passing from this world. Father Wutz and Father Rothschild surely were in danger of such a fate.

I was fortunate in 1950 to meet and interview Father Odo Staudinger, O.S.B. from Wels, Austria. He was a longtime friend of my uncle, Prof. Dr. Sebastian Vogl (a priest), and of my aunts. I met him while he was visiting them in their home in Altötting. We enjoyed a most interesting exchange of information concerning Therese. Father Staudinger was a trusted acquaintance of Therese, as well as a friend of the Bishop of Regensburg—and he knew so much from personal experiences. Also, he, too, wrote a book, a very accurate report on the life of Therese. During conversations with the Bishop of Regensburg, Father Staudinger had learned that the Bishop was squarely behind Therese.

Years before, Therese had told Father Staudinger that Hitler's regime would meet its downfall. She foretold this in 1940, when the Hitler party was solid in their saddle. The downfall came in 1945. Father Staudinger was arrested, like so many of the Konnersreuth circle, and he spent four cruel years in the notorious concentration camp in Dachau.

Elsewhere in this book I have described my meeting with Miss Anni Spiegl shortly before her death from cancer. Anni had been a friend of Therese for thirty years. She gave me valuable pictures, many of which appear in this book, as well as a most interesting description of some of Therese's visions, which also appears herein. I feel very grateful to Anni Spiegl. Surely my meeting with her was providential.

— *Chapter 23* —

VISITS TO GERMANY IN 1973 AND 1975— MEETING WITH FIVE FRIENDS OF THERESE NEUMANN

During the time between Therese's death in 1962 and 1973, I was more or less inactive in my investigation of the case of Therese Neumann. Most of the important occurrences after her death were not known to me at all. I did not even know that the investigative process had been ordered by the Bishop of Regensburg in 1971. To my knowledge, no paper or source in this country ever mentioned this important fact to its readers. The long hours and activities connected with my work hindered me from following up to my satisfaction what I had started in 1927. Then came my retirement from work in 1973. This gave me the opportunity to make a visit to Germany in 1973 with my wife, our son and daughter-in-law.

One of the first visits I made after arriving at my brother's home in Altötting, Bavaria, was to an old-time friend of mine, who was also a dear friend of my uncles (particularly of Uncle Adalbert, who had been executed by the Gestapo). This man was Msgr. Ludwig Uttlinger, who was then, and still is, choir director of the National Shrine of Bavaria. Our meeting was a very pleasant one. He knew about my friendship with Therese, and it did not take very long for him to open a door for me that I did not know existed. I was told that Archbishop Dr. Andreas Rohracher, most eminent retired Archbishop of Salzburg, Austria, was now living in Altötting. Msgr. Uttlinger knew how many important people I had interviewed in the case of Therese Neumann, and this gave me an opportunity to continue where I had left off.

In May of 1973 my wife and I were accorded an appointment with the Archbishop. We had an hour-long discussion regarding Therese Neumann which we will never forget. At the end of the interview the Archbishop told me that the investigative process for the beatification of Therese had been opened by his friend, the Bishop of Regensburg. That was the first time I had heard that good news. He immediately called the Bishop of Regensburg, who in turn gave my name to a priest by the name of Dr. Carl Sträter, S.J., who was in charge of the investigative process on Therese.

Five days later I received an urgent call from Father Sträter stating that he would be in Altötting within a few hours. Upon his arrival, my wife and I met him to discuss Therese's case. After our conversation, he set up his tape recorders, microphones, etc., and for two hours I gave a deposition which included my knowledge and experiences concerning Therese Neumann.

In September, 1975 I again returned to Bavaria, determined to get even more facts about Therese. The first call I made was to Father Sträter, who had his headquarters in Rottenburg, Bavaria. Within a few days I was there for a two-day visit which was a great joy to me, and most enlightening.

The priest insisted that we drive to Eichstätt to see Miss Anni Spiegl, who had been a personal friend of Therese for over thirty years. From the hotel in Eichstätt, Father Sträter gave her a call; he received the surprising news that she was bedridden, very seriously ill, but that in spite of this she would be most happy to see both of us. We visited with her for over two hours, and the information imparted and courtesy extended to us were absolutely the greatest. We were sad to hear that she had cancer and that she was not expected to live more than two months. This we could hardly believe, as she spoke so enthusiastically about her friendship with Therese. It was Anni Spiegl who gave me the great gift of so many pictures that I am now privileged to use in this book. Miss Spiegl's descriptions of some of Therese's visions are also given in this volume.

After our long visit, we departed with a mixture of emotions regarding this courageous lady. Her unwavering faith and complete acceptance of God's will surely made her a most worthy person to be a close friend of Therese for over thirty years. We drove back to Rottenburg, and the following day I returned to Altötting, where so much work was in store for me.

I wish to express my heartfelt thanks to five of Therese's friends who were especially kind to me and who sacrificed much to grant me their time for interviews. The names of the five people who helped me so much during my last and final interviews are: Miss Anni Spiegl, Eichstätt, Bavaria; Father Konstanz Wolfgruber, O.F.M. Cap., Monastery of St. Konrad, Altötting, Bavaria; Msgr. Christian Kunz, retired, Altötting, Bavaria; Miss Maria Meier, retired home economics teacher, Altötting, Bavaria; and Dr. Joseph Mittendorfer, M.D., Munich, Bavaria.

The combined number of years of friendship with Therese Neumann which these five people experienced would no doubt run over one hundred years. Msgr. Kunz had known Therese from childhood. He was a professor at the Regensburg diocesan college all his life. Miss Meier had been a close friend of the mystic for over seven years, and had stayed in the Neumann home many times. She was extremely knowledgeable, as were all the others. Father Konstanz Wolfgruber had not known Therese too long, but he had been appointed by his superior in Altötting to conduct a parish mission in Konnersreuth in 1961. In this capacity he had come into close contact with the mystic. Father Konstanz said he could not remember anyone in all his years to have been so devout and holy toward the will of God as was Therese Neumann. He was extremely impressed by her extraordinary piety, humility, sincerity and spirituality. During the mission Father Konstanz was her confessor. Before they finished the week-long mission, Therese Neumann had made her last general confession.

I took the train to Munich and visited a good friend of

mine from my childhood, Ernst Zettler, who offered to drive me in his car to visit the various important people I had to see—one of whom was Dr. Mittendorfer, who was to grant me a most extraordinary interview. Dr. Mittendorfer had been a long-time medical advisor in the life of Therese Neumann. Although there were other physicians who had seen Therese, Dr. Mittendorfer had been especially close to her. He was known to call himself "Therese's chauffeur" because he was always ready, willing and able to take time out from his arduous medical practice in Munich to go to Konnersreuth and drive Therese anywhere she had to go.

I telephoned Dr. Mittendorfer's home and was told by an attendant that he had had a stroke and was bedridden in serious condition. He was in his 80's. After consulting the doctor, I was told to come anyway; he would be delighted to talk to me.

Mr. Zettler and I drove to his residence; we found Dr. Mittendorfer in bed and partially paralyzed, but he was not to be denied an hour's visit with me. He remembered me as having driven Therese, Father Naber and my wife to his home in Munich in 1950, where we stayed for about four hours. Then, too, the doctor remembered my uncles, and that was enough to grant me a most enlightening interview.

After the visit, Mr. Zettler and I sat down and typed a sort of deposition as a record of our conversation. One statement which Dr. Mittendorfer had made impressed me especially: "If anyone does not believe in Therese Neumann, that person should at least leave her alone." So spoke a man who knew Therese probably better than anyone living. He repeated it several times during our conversation with as much emphasis as he could muster up in his condition—possibly from his deathbed.

Regarding Anni Spiegl, I am sorry to say that she died on October 23, 1975, just a month and ten days after she had told us, from her deathbed, that she would live less than two months. Her death was peaceful, as her sister wrote me, and she was completely resigned to the will of God. May her soul rest in peace.

I feel very humble in the knowledge that I must have had heavenly help from Therese in order to time my visit to Bavaria so perfectly that I was able to talk with these wonderful friends of hers before they passed to their eternal reward. A few weeks later it would have been too late.

— *Chapter 24* —

CRITICS OF THERESE NEUMANN

At this time I find it important enough to look quickly at some of the people who were "detractors" or critics of Therese Neumann. It is important to note that since the Catholic Church has authorized the investigation process for Therese's possible beatification, some measure of approval has already been accorded her life and mystical experiences. It might seem unnecessary, therefore, even to mention her critics, but it is being done because they did influence many people and caused Therese, her family and Father Naber much unhappiness—even if sometimes unknowingly, and with sincere intentions.

Everyone who has studied Therese's case has surely come upon names such as Hilda Graef, Father Siwek, S.J., Dr. Deutsch and Rev. Dr. J. Hanauer. Father Siwek, a Jesuit priest, was one of the earlier personalities who absolutely could not believe in what was going on in Konnersreuth. Father Siwek went to Konnersreuth with other Jesuits back in the 1920's; all except Father Siwek were in favor of the mystical happenings surrounding Therese Neumann. He was always critical, and refused to enter the house to see Therese with his colleagues. He had made up his own mind about the case. Father Siwek's theories and reasons have been disproved, but still, since his book was written by a priest, many Catholics accepted it as the decision of the Church—which it was not. (Unfortunately, Father Siwek was the person chosen to write the article on Therese Neumann in the *New Catholic Encyclopedia*.)

Another widely read critic of Therese in the English-speaking world in the 1950's was Hilda Graef, a college professor. She presented to her readers the possibilities of hysteria (a psychic disturbance which manifests itself in physical phenomena), psychological illness, semi-conscious fraud, and, at best, the idea that Therese's life was full of dubious tendencies. In the book Hilda Graef quoted other sources and then made a sort of analysis of Therese's experiences. (I have been told that she later retracted what she had written.)

I bought Hilda Graef's book back in the 1950's in Omaha, Nebraska and immediately classified it correctly as ill-advised, containing fabrications, throwing grave doubt on Therese's reputation. I thus considered it uncharitable in the highest degree.

In 1953 I made a trip to Konnersreuth and on October 16 had a long discussion with Therese, Father Naber and Therese's father, Ferdinand Neumann. Therese told me point blank that she did not know Hilda Graef, that she would not recognize her if she walked through the door, and that her book consisted of lies and misrepresentations, etc., etc. Hilda Graef may have been in Konnersreuth, but I learned that there was no personal meeting with Therese in any way, shape or form. Upon my questioning Therese as to why a lawsuit had never been filed (I told her that I would have done so), she promptly told me that against ordinary lies she could not afford to file suit; if she did so she would be in court more than in Konnersreuth. However, she pointed out that if anyone questioned her moral character, then she had to clear herself, and she had done so on several occasions.

Despite the very misleading picture presented in Hilda Graef's book, many readers, including some priests, accepted it. In fact, I personally have read an article in a publication for priests, based on the above-mentioned book, in which Therese Neumann was described as a very questionable character; such words as "swindle" and "hysteria" were used. It was advised that priests should be "very cautious" about believing in what went on in Konnersreuth.

Of course, the majority of people have always believed in Therese, but when negative articles and books receive the Imprimatur, as Hilda Graef's book did, they naturally carry some weight in people's minds, for many consider a book so marked to be an authoritative statement by the Church—which is not the case. An Imprimatur simply indicates that a book has been judged to contain nothing contrary to Catholic faith or morals. Even when an author later retracts what he or she has written, the harm is already done and is difficult to undo.

For me, in particular, the results of Hilda Graef's book were devastating. My own booklet on Therese Neumann, which I wrote in 1956, was refused an Imprimatur, I could not advertise it in diocesan papers, and, of course, no Catholic bookstore would take it. This opposition notwithstanding, the booklet gave a true and accurate picture of Therese Neumann. In fact, I would be ashamed of myself if my writing on the case were less than 99% accurate.

In Bavaria in 1953 I found out very quickly that Hilda Graef's book is disregarded there. No one ever worries about it in the least bit. One theologian who had known Therese Neumann since childhood tried to pacify me with this advice: Christ had His enemies, they put Him to death—so what are you complaining about? I complain no more. Therese Neumann can stand on her own record and she needs no help from me.

Some years ago a medical expert, Dr. Deutsch, who seemed to be sincerely interested in obtaining the facts about Therese's experiences, made a private investigation of Therese. Dr. Deutsch was accorded the courtesy to see for himself, to investigate the mystic, to interview, and to examine and do whatever was proper in order to evaluate Therese's unusual experiences. All this was done in a very dignified and professional manner. After this was concluded, Dr. Deutsch had a meeting with Therese and Father Naber, and both were satisfied with the true findings of this eminent medical doctor. They parted as friends, to the satisfaction of all concerned.

Months later, Dr. Deutsch came out with a book which was contrary and falsified in every respect. He pictured Therese as a charlatan and a deceiver and made slanderous accusations completely at variance with his friendly, sympathetic manner while he was in Konnersreuth. Years went by, while Therese and Father Naber had to swallow this bitter pill with anguish.

Then, on his deathbed, Dr. Deutsch wrote a letter to Father Naber in which he retracted and repudiated everything he had written about the mystic. He apologized most abjectly and penitently, and openly confessed that he himself believed Therese's case to be genuine and utterly inexplicable on natural grounds. He had done Therese a great injustice in order to satisfy his superiors at the university; they demanded an adverse criticism of the case of Therese Neumann or else Dr. Deutsch would have lost his position at the university. On his deathbed, he seized the opportunity to right the serious wrong he had done. Therese, Father Naber and Therese's father told me this in a long interview in 1953.

Following the death of Therese Neumann, another very strong critic appeared on the scene in the person of Dr. Joseph Hanauer, a priest of the diocese of Regensburg and also a teacher in a church-related prep school in Regensburg. In his book he mentions the word "hysteria" many times and he, too, believed that the events of Konnersreuth were a swindle and of controversial nature.

Regarding Father Hanauer's book, one of the Vice Postulators of Therese's process, Rev. Dr. Carl Sträter, S.J., wrote to me: "Due to the 1950 book, and now Hanauer's, we know that Bishops, clergy and the laity may have an unfavorable opinion regarding Therese Neumann. Probably they are influenced by the book of J. Hanauer, *Konnersreuth als Testfall* [*Konnersreuth as Test Case*], Munich, 1972. The author is a priest of the diocese of Regensburg and very much against Therese Neumann. He is, however, very biased. He collected everything that he could interpret in a negative sense or that he means to be open to an unfavorable interpretation. He is blind to everything else. To some who know nothing of Therese Neumann, his work may give the impression of being written by a scientist (long bibliography, many notes), but to persons who have known Therese N. well or to persons who have studied the case objectively, his book has no great value." So speak Regensburg and Konnersreuth.

I would like to ask Father Hanauer just why he would classify Therese as "hysterical." Is it because she lived exclusively on the Sacred Host for over thirty-six years? Is it because she carried the wound marks of Christ on her body and bled profusely at times, or because she spoke ancient languages perfectly? Is that hysteria? Or is it hysteria that for a lifetime Therese fed the poor and visited the sick as one of her Christian projects? Is that hysteria? Or is it that Therese was influential in building a seminary and a Carmelite convent in Konnersreuth? Is that hysteria? Of course, no one can explain by scientific means the events in the life of Therese Neumann.

Opposition is a way of life. Our Lord was the victim of it in His day, and it will remain with us for all time.

In my interviews with so many priests, in particular, I found a similar situation as with these authors. These people were all of high intellect and they were good educators, but when it came to mystical and unusual happenings they found themselves lost in the woods. They believed nothing unless they could find an answer in a laboratory, in a textbook or by some scientific means. If such an answer was not forthcoming, then it must be "hysteria."

Many of Therese's detractors spent very little or no time in Konnersreuth, nor did Father Hanauer ever talk to Therese or Father Naber. In fact, although Father Hanauer was a priest of the diocese of Regensburg, he never saw Therese or Father Naber, and he never even went to Konnersreuth. He apparently felt that there was no need to go there, since the whole thing was a swindle anyway. That is the sort of thing that the friends of Konnersreuth have had to live with. I have tried, by writing this book, to counteract in some small way some of the wrong that has been done. These are very materialistic times, and people are not as concerned about mystical happenings as they were at some times in the past when there was more faith in God.

Many of the very critical articles on Therese were printed in the German left-wing press. They tried desperately to ridicule Therese and make it appear that the stigmata was just sort of a hypnotical show-type talent which surfaces everywhere now and then. No Catholic paper in Germany has ever printed such a position, and they have always rejected any form of comparison with showman-type performances.

In contrast to the German Catholic press, I have an article before me, written in 1960 and published in a U.S. national Catholic weekly, in which an article concerning mystics appeared. It included the following:

> I know of three [stigmatists]. There is a Capuchin Padre Pio, who I think is authentic. There is Therese Neumann of Konnersreuth in Bavaria. The late Archbishop Noll used to swear by her, but Father Henry McAnulty C.S.Sp., now President of Duquesne University, once told me that he visited her when he was an army chaplain and he was far from satisfied. Her bishop has asked her to submit to a medical examination, but on the advice of her father and (or) pastor, she has refused. That's enough for me.
>
> And then there is a rather ordinary character up in Hamburg, not a Catholic, not especially holy, who has what appears to be the stigmata and who finds them an awful nuisance. "Don't know why I should be bothered," he mutters to his cronies. "I just wish the darned things would go away." It seems that the blood from the palms of his hands keeps getting into his beer.

This is not the first time I have read ridiculous articles, but I was dismayed that such as this would be published in a national Catholic weekly in the United States. Therese and Father Pio have often been compared, but then to compare either one with a very dubious charlatan from show business in Hamburg, who fooled the world on purpose for a very short time, I find utterly disrespectful and in very bad taste. The author of the article evidently knew little or nothing about

Therese Neumann or the man from Hamburg. Be that as it may, the fact remains that the author of that article is responsible for his actions and I am responsible for mine.

In one particular instance Therese herself dealt with one of her critics in person. A well-known university professor who had examined Therese went into an unusual explanation for her enlightenment. "First of all," he said, "the Friday bleedings are caused by 'autosuggestion.'" She did not know what that word meant, so he explained it as follows: "Year in and year out, you imagine that you have the wound marks of Christ on your body and that the wounds bleed. Thereupon the wounds do actually appear and bleed." Therese listened to all of that very attentively, without saying a word. After the professor had finished what he evidently regarded as a profound analysis, he settled back to await Therese's reaction. It came as follows: "You must be a very brilliant man, otherwise you would not be a professor at a university. Now, I will ask you to begin to imagine, day in and day out, that you are an ox; you also imagine you have received horns. Then, all of a sudden, you find to your amazement that that is actually what you are!" The professor departed without saying a word.

If one could only have the complete record of the abuses, denunciations, lies and accusations that were written and said about Therese, one would indeed be greatly shocked. Most of the accusations that I have personally read in papers and magazines are so shameful or even diabolical that I will not mention them in my writings. Therese let all this pass outwardly unnoticed, and quietly inside she asked Our Lord to place sufferings upon her for the forgiveness of those who wrote these things. Only violent abuses such as defamation of morals and character were not handled in such a manner. (The socialist and Communist press were in the forefront in making slanderous statements.) Therese won lawsuits in courts in Berlin, Paris and in other cities.

Here it may be well to mention an unfortunate incident which occurred in 1927, when two young skeptics came to

Konnersreuth to see Therese. They did not believe what they had heard about her. As they were sitting in the local inn, the waiter overheard their conversation. It was highly critical and derogatory; they both were of the opinion that the "people who believe in such nonsense must be crazy." That same day, both became violent themselves and had to be taken to an institution in straightjackets. Investigation showed no trace of insanity in either man's family.

I am rather amused by an article I have before me in which the assumption is made that Therese took food while no one was around. Therese did not take any food since 1922, and since 1926 neither food nor drink in any shape or form. Furthermore, she had no desire to eat. No substance would even stay in her body, except the Holy Eucharist. Even a drop of water that might trickle down her throat while Therese was brushing her teeth was immediately ejected, as though by divine power. The history of the Church contains many authentic accounts of mystics who required little or even no food. Yet they did not become emaciated as ordinary people would, but were of normal weight.

Reading further in this article, I find that the problem is finally "solved" regarding the blood which flowed from Therese's wounds during ecstatic visions. The writer self-satisfyingly finds that this blood, upon examination, proved to be menstrual blood! (And bleeding from the eyes is spoken of as rather common in hysterical women.)

This is completely false, since Therese Neumann had no natural discharges from her body since 1930! When I read the malicious accusations made against Therese, I cannot help recalling the slogan which the infamous Hitler used: "Lie all you care to—among the many you will always find believers."

It has been said that Therese could not possibly have been a saint because she did not receive the wounds all at one time, she lived too modernly, she did not sleep on a hard bed, etc., etc. First, I wish to make it very clear that neither Therese, nor her family, nor Father Naber, nor anyone close to her has ever referred to her as a saint. This is not for us to decide, and when the proper time comes, the Catholic Church will make the decision in the matter. In the meantime, I have never heard that there is any one specific pattern one must follow in order to become a faithful servant of our Lord and Master. It is my personal conviction that Therese suffered more in her simple bed in a few minutes of ecstasy than many of her critics do in a lifetime.

Some of Therese's critics seem to feel that Father Naber was responsible for what was happening in Konnersreuth. They believe that the priest may have transmitted messages to Therese by "mental telepathy." How Father Naber, or anyone else, could transmit something to another person that he did not know himself, has never been explained. The languages, for instance, which Therese used during the ecstasies, were studied for weeks by experts before the experts were able to make their reports. Father Naber would have been the first to laugh at such a questionable tribute given him.

I think back to the days of 1927 and the first onslaught of the critics. Perhaps they have been hoping that something would happen to vindicate their theories and assumptions. These critics have waited a long time, but in vain. In like manner, this will be true of today's skeptics, who foolishly try to fit mystical experiences into a test tube. The modern "scientific" approach to the problem of analyzing Therese is as destitute of verification as were the wishful opinions of skeptical predecessors.

The evidence put forth in this book proves that Therese Neumann was always obedient to her parents, her pastor, her Bishop and the dean of the Catholic hierarchy in Munich. All of them were her best friends.

Moreover, there have been many books written which are very favorable to Therese. Whether these books were authored by priest, professor or layman, I have found no instance of anyone writing favorably about Therese Neumann who had not spent hours, months or years with her—and in some instances even a lifetime of friendship with the mystic. In my case, it took me over forty-five years of ardent private study before I decided to write what I knew of Therese.

Among the many favorable books about Therese, I shall name but a few; they are those by Archbishop Dr. Carl Gaspar, Archbishop Joseph Teodorowicz, Bishop Sigismund Waitz of Salzburg, Anni Spiegl (at least three books), Dr. Josef Klosa, Dr. (Med.) Hans Fröhlich and Dr. Fritz Gerlich of Munich. Dr. Gerlich had been a skeptic and ridiculer of anything supernatural, but upon doing an honest—and lengthy—firsthand investigation, he became convinced of Therese's genuineness, became a close friend of Therese, Father Naber, and the Neumann family, and converted to the Catholic Faith.

The end result of all this is the fact that the friends of Konnersreuth outnumber the opponents to such a great degree that the skeptics should not even be mentioned. My wife and I classify ourselves as ordinary, simple people. And yet in calculating the extent of our acquaintance with Therese Neumann in research for a 280-minute tape in English that we presented to Father Sträter, we accurately came up with at least 205 hours that we had spent with Therese Neumann and/or Father Naber, or with Ferdinand Neumann, Sr. This includes shopping, driving, visiting, interviewing, etc., etc. Of course we too belong to the mile-long list of the *friends of Therese Neumann.*

I would like to direct a few conciliatory words to our brothers and sisters who, perhaps even unknowingly and through no fault of their own, have joined the ranks of the detractors. With incorrect information being spread around, this could easily happen. To these I say: read what genuine witnesses have written about Therese's life, and you will see the truth.

The life Therese had to live as a mystic and stigmatist in Konnersreuth, following the will of God, was a life of pain and suffering. Yet it was always a joy for her to do all that, "if only it is the will of God." With those words one could summarize her whole life story.

I would like to point out the fact that now 90 witnesses (including myself) have been interrogated in the investigations leading up to Therese Neumann's beatification process. Upon my question to Father Sträter as to when the opponents would have a chance to be similarly treated, he told me, "No one stepped forward"—not a single person. That should put the subject in a different light. We lost some small "battles"— but we are winning the "war!"

— *Chapter 25* —

CONCLUSION: THE GENUINENESS OF THERESE NEUMANN'S MYSTICAL EXPERIENCES

The opinions rendered on the supernatural occurrences in Konnersreuth by eminent ecclesiastical authorities, as well as by medical scientists, scholars and people interested in the case, have pointed to the fact that they cannot be explained by natural causes. What happened to Therese was not a mere medical problem, as some would assume, but rather a religious phenomenon. Not only the miracle of inedia (living without food), but hundreds of preternatural happenings during all those years are each miracles in themselves, for which an explanation on the natural level has not been found.

I have at times asked a simple and reasonable question: How long would it take for a person living in your town, or anywhere in the United States, to be detected as a fraud if he falsely claimed to need no food whatever in order to live? The answers given to this question have not been startling: from a few days to several months. Following this line of thinking, consider further that this person did not live a quiet, inactive life, or even a life confined to his home, but rather saw thousands of visitors each month, worked around the house, and was active in the community, besides being constantly with his parents, brothers and sisters. Furthermore, consider that he was examined hundreds of times by doctors, scholars and professional people, and lived under the scrutiny of the entire community.

How long could such a person claim the miracle of inedia if it were not true? Not very long, you say? Then why should the village of Konnersreuth, Bavaria, be any different from any other community in the world? Therese lived in Konnersreuth, taking an active part in civic affairs, working among people and doing everything that is expected of any good, loyal citizen. Therese Neumann stood this rigid test for nearly thirty-six years! This fact should not be overlooked when we answer the accusations of her detractors.

During September of 1950, when I was with Therese and Father Naber on a trip, our activities were similar to those of anyone on vacation. We attended Mass together, visited churches and cemeteries, traveled, shopped, visited a shrine and a museum, and had long visits with family and friends. The schedule was heavy and the strain was felt by Father Naber, as well as by my wife and myself. Yet Therese was ever fresh and alert and never showed any sign of fatigue during the entire trip. I do not say this lightly, but Therese could wear out many people trying to keep up with her in her daily activities.

After talking to hundreds of people in the area of Konnersreuth, including the mayor of the village on many occasions, I know that these fine people, many of whom have known Therese since her birth, are very devoted to her, do not doubt her genuineness, and regard her as the outstanding citizen of their community because of her noble character, her high degree of devotion to everything that is good and uplifting, and her never-ending acts of charity in visiting the sick and assisting those who need help. This was especially apparent after World War II, when so much help for displaced persons came from the hands of Therese Neumann. She told me personally that this was made possible by the prayers of her friends all over the world, and the many donations of food and clothing and CARE packages she received, particularly from the American people. These gifts of all kinds were distributed by Therese to the needy of all faiths.

Therese told me that the pastors of Lutheran parishes in nearby towns came to her and personally thanked her, and expressed the appreciation of the displaced persons and others who had shared in her generosity. The fact that she could be helpful in alleviating the sufferings of so many made Therese very happy. This was emphasized when she and Father Naber requested that I convey their thanks and appreciation to all those in this part of the world who had so generously donated food and clothing for her to distribute where the need was the greatest.

I have before me an article from a West Coast newspaper in which the case of Therese Neumann is called a "riddle." In my estimation, it is unjust to denominate the mystical occurrences of Konnersreuth by that word. Therese Neumann was either a complete fraud, or she was one of the people chosen by God to possess certain rare mystical gifts. It seems that if she were a fraud, after thirty-six years of scrutiny the Church would have taken the proper action to ban visitors from seeing her. Instead, her long list of admirers among dignitaries of the Church is ever increasing.

The late beloved Cardinal Michael von Faulhaber, Archbishop of Munich and Freising and Dean of the German Catholic hierarchy, demonstrated his belief in Therese's genuineness by offering the Holy Sacrifice of the Mass many times on the little altar in her bedroom. The same was done by Cardinal Kaspar of Prague, Cardinal Preysing of Berlin, and many other Bishops and Archbishops. We can safely assume that these learned men were completely informed, by the good offices of the Bishop of Regensburg, of the life of Therese Neumann and the preternatural occurrences of Konnersreuth. During her life Therese Neumann had always been in contact with and surrounded by hundreds of the very best theologians and professionals, members of the secular clergy, of the German Catholic Bishops Conference, and of the monastic life.

Elsewhere in this book is found the position taken by the ecclesiastical authority of the diocese of Regensburg, in which the parish of Konnersreuth is located. There was never any official ban on visiting Therese. In the fall of 1953, I met Father Odo Staudinger, O.S.B., a Benedictine priest from Salzburg, Austria, while he was visiting my uncle in Altötting.

He is the author of a booklet on Therese, which he wrote many years ago, and he has followed the case with the greatest interest. I asked him how the Bishop of Regensburg regards Konnersreuth. He assured me: "The Bishop of Regensburg told me personally, 'I am all in favor of Therese Neumann.'"

The many priests in Bavaria with whom I have talked about Therese have all been wholeheartedly in favor of the mystic. They have assured me that nothing ever occurred in the mystical life of Therese which is in the least way contrary to the teachings of the Catholic Church. The opinions of these many priests carry much weight in forming one's opinion about Konnersreuth; but the one that overshadows all the others is Pope Pius XII, who sent his personal greetings to Therese, which she received in my presence. For me this leaves no doubt of the genuineness and divine origin of the happenings in Konnersreuth.

Was Therese Neumann hysterical? She had none of the symptoms of hysteria, as she was a normal, robust woman who faced life with a fearlessness that was absolutely heroic. It seems to me that some scoffers at the mystical life, who cannot accept the miraculous, merely classify such persons as hysterical. Perhaps there has never been a true mystic who has not been so accused. Do such detractors think that the German hierarchy and even civil authorities of Bavaria would let such a "fraud" go on for almost thirty-six years without labeling the person as a fake? I do not think so. The training of these high-ranking authorities of the Catholic Church puts them in a far better position to evaluate the spiritual characteristics of Therese Neumann than someone who has not had such training. They would, indeed, have been the first to tell us if her experiences conflicted with the teachings of the Catholic Church.

Did Therese refuse further investigation? The truth is that Therese never refused to comply with any order coming from the proper ecclesiastical authority or her pastor and spiritual director to subject herself to medical investigation or examination. No such request was made since the summer of 1927, when Therese was under observation every second of the day and night for a period of fifteen days. (See Chapter 13.) One can be very safe in assuming that the resulting report was 100 percent favorable to Therese. It is on record in the Bishop's office at Regensburg, the office which requested the examination, and there is no reason to believe that the outcome of this observation is not known to the proper ecclesiastical offices of other dioceses and to the Vatican. Further examinations would have added no more convincing proof than that already established.

If it had ever become necessary to further prove the genuineness of Therese's mystical phenomena, we may be sure that no one would have had to urge the proper authorities who had jurisdiction over Konnersreuth to open an investigation which would be as complete as possible. But as Mr. Neumann pointed out to me, if they had let everyone make his own investigations, Therese would have been pushed from one clinic to another; and since no one was ever able to explain the phenomena, it would have become a competition of different ideas between one group of doctors and another.

In all humility, and in obedience to the will of God, Therese and all the Neumann family would rather have been left alone to live their lives. They always discouraged any show or sensationalism concerning what had happened to their own Therese. Although people who went to Konnersreuth with a sincere desire to see Therese were never turned away if it was at all possible to grant visits, nevertheless, no one was ever urged by the Neumanns to come to them. In Konnersreuth one cannot find any sign of commercialism. Even though hundreds of thousands of visitors had been there in the past four decades, the first characteristics one noted upon meeting Therese were simplicity and humility.

I am reluctant to believe that the Saviour would give to an hysterical person such divine characteristics as He bestowed upon Therese, especially her gift of recognizing holy and blessed articles and the Eucharistic Sacrament even at a distance, as well as the consecrated hands of a priest. Nor do I believe that He would permit an hysterical person to suffer His Passion, or that He would reveal to such a person the details of His life and those of the saints, as well as the languages they spoke. The stigmata, the miracle of inedia, Therese's miraculous cures from illness and blindness, the untold number of converts to the Catholic Church, can only lead me to repeat with Therese her desire: "*Damit die Welt erkenne dass es ein höheres Wesen gibt!*" (That the world will recognize the existence of a higher Being!).

Writing to me in 1983, Father Sträter, one of the two Vice-Postulators in Therese's process, stated: "In my opinion Therese Neumann is certainly relevant for our modern times: Her great love of Christ, her readiness to suffer with Him, her great love for the Eucharist make her a person who is an example for our times. St. Francis did not become a saint simply because he loved the sun, the animals, etc., but because of his love of Christ, of his poverty, his cross, etc."

In a letter to me in 1984, Father Sträter lamented the disbelief in Therese Neumann which prevails among many priests in the United States. He wrote, "It really is a pity that in the U.S.A. there exists such opposition against the case of Therese Neumann. But in our days the sense of the supernatural diminishes everywhere, and it is for the Church a very difficult time. Therefore, it is not to be wondered at that also in the U.S.A. many priests are *a priori* against 'Resl' ['Resl' was Therese Neumann's nickname]."

Here I will quote a little article which an American priest, Father Victor Wilkiemeyer, pastor of St. Lawrence parish in Santa Clara, California, published in his parish bulletin of February 13, 1983. Father Wilkiemeyer had met Therese Neumann personally, and he was convinced that she was a person who had been "given by God to inspire you and me."

Dear Parishioner:

It was so rare as a youth for me to read in an Oklahoma newspaper anything complimentary about the Catholic religion; thus, it was almost with an obsession that annually, on Holy Saturday morning, I would scan the local morning paper looking for a report on Therese Neumann, to discover if she had gone through the Passion of Christ. Invariably every year, somewhere on an inside page there would be a short report from Munich, Germany that Therese Neumann, living in the village of Konnersreuth, again had [suffered the Passion], and that the crowds were becoming a problem for the government. It was one of those rare moments that deep inside I felt like saying to my little world, "She's a Catholic!"

As time passed, I read a moving pamphlet written by an American woman who visited her. It was [like] reading of some impossible dream. Then, during the Second World War, Catholic chaplains would return and report on her unbelievable life. Never in my wildest dreams did I think I would ever see this mysterious woman with the wounds of Christ who had taken no nourishment, including water, since 1926 (until her very death in 1962); whose existence was feared by Adolf Hitler (whom she defied). In 1957 when I planned a visit to Europe, I heard of a man in San Jose who had known her personally, even wrote a book on her. (The latest up-dated version is available at the parish house for $5.00.) I was determined to meet him. Through a mutual friend I met and spent an evening with him; he even promised to have his brother meet our group in Munich and take us to her village. Actually, when we arrived in Munich, who was at the airport but my new friend himself, Albert Vogl! He was determined I would meet Therese. Believe it or not, to make a long story short, I not only met her, spoke with her, but offered Mass in her parish church (St. Lawrence, Martyr), which Mass she attended.

What is so ironic is that today in America, Therese Neumann's life is shunned by Catholic leaders, even ridiculed; she was a "psycho." "Some nut," etc., has been their rebuttal of her fantastic life!

No one who has ever met Therese Neumann has concluded anything but that she was a living miracle of God. The only critics—I repeat, the ONLY critics—are people who have never even met her! When we saw her, there were notices all over the village that the Bishop had permitted her request that no one be given an audience with her without permission of her pastor. She once, at the peak of her fame, threatened to move if a hotel was built in the village; nor were curio and souvenir shops permitted. Yet, her critics accused her of being a "fame seeker."

In her lifetime she was known and admired by the leading churchmen of Europe; both Popes Pius XI and XII sent her a personal blessing without being requested to do so; Cardinals Faulhaber and Preysing not only knew her but wrote articles endorsing and lauding her. Three years ago Pope John Paul sent Cardinal Seper, Secretary of the Congregation of the Faith, to her diocese to set in motion the process of her canonization as a saint. My good friend, "Herr" Vogl, recently received an official letter from the Diocese of Regensburg (her diocese) informing him that official "Implementation of the Information Process" was underway and would he testify?

The great mystery to me has always been: Why are American churchmen and writers so damning in their attitude toward Therese Neumann, whom they never met or saw; yet, European Cardinals, Bishops, theologians, even Popes speak of her as something special from God? God only knows how much we need someone like Therese to inspire America today—yet, we shun her; perhaps her eventual canonization to sainthood might change their minds???

> Sincerely,
> Father Wilkiemeyer

If what you have read in this book has convinced you that I unhesitatingly believe in and defend the genuineness and the heroic life of Therese Neumann, then I say to you: "You are absolutely correct!" I am happy to belong to the "Konnersreuth Circle," a phrase intended by some to be derogatory, but which really denotes a unique privilege. I love everything that Konnersreuth represents, and I thank God I have been given the gift of faith in Him and the discernment to recognize His special presence in Konnersreuth.

I know I am not alone in this. Many of the greatest leaders of the Church have paid tribute to Therese, including both Pope Pius XI and Pope Pius XII, who sent their blessings to Therese and gave her precious relics as gifts. "Therese Neumann is for Germany a very extraordinary grace," was the statement made by Bishop Malan of Brazil, South America, after he had visited Therese in Konnersreuth. In his book on Therese Neumann, Bishop Dr. Waitz of Innsbruck, Austria has beautifully expressed my own convictions regarding Therese. I quote from Bishop Waitz:

> I joyfully regard the occurrences of Konnersreuth as of supernatural origin. In this manner, the message of the holy Cross of Calvary is brought to mankind, which is falling more and more into the abyss of materialism of this passing world. In my mind there has never been any doubt about Therese Neumann. I was so impressed, seeing her during the terrible suffering of the Passion, that not even the slightest thought of doubt could enter my mind. Many reliable experts have already discounted the idea of "swindle" and "hysteria." Frequent investigations have given us proof of that. Human science is not in a position to explain what happens in Konnersreuth, for the obvious reason that it lies outside the natural law and natural comprehension. The case of Therese Neumann is, therefore, not a mere medical problem, as some would assume, but a constant and consistent series of religious phenomena. It will eventually fall within the jurisdiction of the Catholic Church to make a decision.

The late Cardinal Michael von Faulhaber, brilliant and courageous Archbishop of Munich and Freising and Dean of the German hierarchy, spoke these words regarding Therese Neumann in a Lenten sermon:

Men of today, return to the devotion of the suffering of Our Lord Jesus Christ. Depart from the materialism of our modern age and seek refuge within the sacred wounds of our Redeemer. This humble child of the Bavarian hills has wholly submitted her soul unto Christ's sufferings, particularly on the Fridays which serve us constantly as a reminder of the Passion of Our Lord. Out of pity for His suffering she has shed bloody tears and thereby assumed a living image of the Crucified. Like St. Paul, she, too, wants to know only the crucified Saviour, and like St. Bonaventure, this child of the simple village school has derived her knowledge from the book of the Cross.

Like a speechless preacher, through this example, and regardless of the final disposition of the case, she has brought Europe's people beneath the Cross of Christ and placed it into His Sacred Wounds, from which the redemption and reconciliation with the Father have found their source. In reference to the only feast which is dedicated to a stigmatic, namely September 17th, the Church reminds us, "Through the wounds of St. Francis, the complacency of our time should be overcome with an increased devotion to the Passion of Christ."

This is the meaning of the message of Konnersreuth: "Pray the Stations of the Cross more frequently and more devoutly and hide yourself within the Wounds of Christ."

Therese Neumann would undoubtedly agree that "the message of Konnersreuth" is the love of the Saviour and of His Cross.

— *Chapter 26* —

CAUSE FOR BEATIFICATION

After the death of Therese Neumann there was a virtual avalanche of requests to the Bishop of Regensburg to start the investigation immediately in the case of Konnersreuth. Such requests came not only from a large number of the hierarchy and clergy, but also from many lay people from all over the world. It should be known by all that Cardinal Bea, S.J., not too long after Therese's death, publicly and on several occasions requested that the case be opened very soon. The Cardinal was then a member of the papal curia in charge of the Ecumenical office at the Vatican. He was a personal friend of Therese and what she stood for.

Since the new canon law went into effect on the first day of Advent, November 27, 1983, much more of the investigative work leading up to beatification is under the jurisdiction of the local bishop, rather than of Rome. Here is a summary of the steps which now must be followed:

1) The *investigative process,* which is conducted by the Bishop and the postulators he appoints. (Actually, the process can be begun by a *pia unio*, a pious association, though after some time the Bishop must of course approve the work of this association.) If the investigative process is concluded successfully, the Bishop continues, according to guidelines from the Vatican, with 2) the *informative process*. This is conducted along the same lines as the investigative process, but goes deeper. It involves the preparation of a document of some hundred pages on the particular Servant of God—on his or her actions, virtues, words, faults, etc. Every witness has to be interrogated about some of these points. This document is called the *Positiones et Artikuli;* it is the hypothesis

needed for the opening of the beatification process. If the informative process, including the *Artikuli*, is successfully concluded in favor of the Servant of God, then the Bishop, at his own discretion, may open the actual 3) *beatification process*. (The permission of Rome is not necessary for the opening of this process.) The beatification process, conducted by the postulators appointed by the Bishop, involves more investigation, as well as the certification of three miracles performed through the intercession of the Servant of God. If the beatification process is concluded successfully, it is followed by 4) *beatification* by the Pope. Then a 5) *cause for canonization* is opened in Rome; this involves investigation by the Sacred Congregation for the Causes of Saints and the certification of three more miracles. If all is concluded successfully, it is followed by 6) *canonization* by the Pope.

In the case of Therese Neumann, the investigative process was opened in 1971 and successfully concluded about ten years later, with Therese coming through with flying colors. Bishop Rudolf Gräber of Regensburg opened the official investigative process, ordering it to be conducted under the direction of Rev. Prof. Dr. Carl Sträter, S.J. Here is a translation of the Bishop's letter which set this process in motion:

From the Bishop of Regensburg   84 Regensburg 1
June 6, 1971

Authorization   Power of Attorney

The Reverend Dr. Carl Sträter is hereby appointed to gather historical evidence of the life of Therese Neumann and to make it available in the form of a portfolio for registration. Permission is hereby given Reverend Father to examine documents which are in safekeeping in Konnersreuth. However, these documents may not be removed from there.

Reverend Father Sträter S.J. is also authorized to interrogate witnesses in the life of Therese Neumann, with ecclesiastical approval. Father is also requested to compile these findings into an official protocol. It is expected that Father Sträter will receive the necessary cooperation.

✝Rudolph
Bishop of Regensburg

On April 28, 1982 Bishop Gräber chose a postulator and two vice-postulators to conduct the informative process. He appointed Rev. Anton Vogl, pastor of St. Lawrence parish in Konnersreuth, to be the postulator; and as vice-postulators, the Bishop appointed Father Carl Sträter, S.J. (from Holland), and Rev. Ulrich Veh, O.F.M. Cap. Father Veh was to be in charge of the *Positiones et Artikuli,* and Father Sträter was to be in charge of the documentation of the investigative and informative processes.

Since the time of these appointments, Father Sträter has retired (in 1986) due to ill health and advanced age, so the new vice-postulator in charge of the documentation department is now Emmeram H. Ritter. Also, in 1986 Bishop Gräber retired; the new Bishop of Regensburg is Rt. Rev. Manfred Müller.

The guidelines for the informative process carried out at the diocesan level are always outlined by the Sacred Congregation for the Causes of Saints in Rome. The outline of the Vatican came in four messages from Rome to Regensburg:

1. The *Constitutio Apostolica*, by Pope Johannes Paulus II, January 25, 1983.
2. The *Normae Servandae in Inquisitionibus ab Episcopis Faciendis in Causis Sanctorum*, February 7, 1983.
3. The *Decretum Generale*, February 7, 1983.
4. The *Regolamento della Sacra Congregazione per le Cause Santi*, March 21, 1983.

The important diocesan document entitled the *Positiones et Artikuli* was finally finished in the spring of 1985. The document consists of five parts, covering Therese's life, heroic virtues, supernatural gifts, death, odor of sanctity and miracles. Upon my visit to Altötting at that time, Father Veh very joyfully showed this 100-page dossier to me and my group.

Finally all this was submitted to the main postulator, Father Anton Vogl, in Konnersreuth. When he has evaluated all the various documents he will turn all over to the Bishop in Regensburg, officially petitioning him for the opening of the beatification process. These various documents include, in addition to the *Positiones et Artikuli*, documents on healings, depositions, handwritten documents by Therese Neumann, and all witnesses' reports connected with the case. The report from Konnersreuth is that the beatification process is expected to be opened soon.

Ninety witnesses from all over the world have given depositions regarding Therese Neumann. These include one witness from North America (myself) and one witness from South America.

In a letter which I received from Father Sträter (dated February 28, 1984), the vice-postulator acknowledged the tapes I had made for the process, as well as a personal meeting in Altötting about ten years previous in which I had told Father Sträter much about Therese Neumann. Regarding this meeting Father Sträter wrote, "I registered all on my tape recorder, and a sister here in town wrote everything down on her typewriter. So you are a very valuable witness in the case of Therese Neumann!"

During the upcoming beatification process about 90 competent witnesses will be called again to give oral testimony before an ecclesiastical court of law. If I am called upon to testify again, I shall be there promptly.

My own official work in the case can be summed up thus: One tape deposition by my wife and myself given before Father Sträter over in Germany in May of 1973 (for the investigative process); three 90-minute tapes in English made in 1983 in Regensburg, Konnersreuth and Eichstätt (interviews of myself, and sometimes also of my wife Esther, by members of the Bishop's tribunal) and turned over to Father Sträter; and two 90-minute tapes in German made in the United States and mailed in February of 1984 to four different recipients: Father Sträter, Father Anton Vogl, Father Veh, and the

Carmelite convent Theresianum in Konnersreuth (for the informative process). Ninety people were called to Germany for the informative process, and I was among the first ten to be asked. In all, my wife and I spent 205 hours with Therese Neumann and/or Father Naber—often also in the company of other family members: Therese's father, her brother August, and her sisters Ottilie and Mary.

The first of the above-mentioned interviews came about after an hour-long discussion which I had with retired Archbishop Andreas Rohracher of Salzburg, Austria. After that memorable discussion, the Archbishop asked my permission to have all that I told him recorded. He then called his friend, Bishop Gräber, who ordered Father Sträter to drive over to Altötting immediately and tape Vogl's information. I have also been asked to send Father Sträter any items handwritten by Therese which I might have; thus I have turned over my letters from her and holy cards signed by her. The cause is receiving such documents from all over the world.

Father Sträter has already established, after intensive investigation, that Therese Neumann's living without food for over 35 years is absolutely true, without any doubt whatsoever. Also, the genuineness of the stigmata has found full recognition by both Church and medical authorities.

Incidentally, in 1984 I met Archbishop Josef Tomko from the Vatican during a trip to Minneapolis; Archbishop Tomko is General Secretary for the Synod of Bishops. I had a long conversation with him regarding Therese Neumann. He agreed with me because he had been informed by his friend Cardinal Seper, who had spent time in Konnersreuth regarding the case of Therese Neumann. Cardinal Seper, from the Prefecture of the Congregation for the Doctrine of the Faith, had been sent from the Vatican to Konnersreuth around 1980.

Our visits with Father Vogl in Konnersreuth have always been most cordial. Father Vogl calls me his "namesake" and is very proud of what I am doing in the States regarding Therese Neumann. He gave us all kinds of time, and we had long visits with him.

Over 300 cures have been credited to the intercession of Therese Neumann, and the number is steadily rising. Fourteen of these have been written up in a very specific manner in the *Positiones et Artikuli*.

During my visit of 1985, Father Vogl offered to describe a couple of the certified miracles attributed to Therese Neumann's intercession. One involved a young boy whose finger had been horribly crushed in an accident. (I saw a photograph of this.) After he and his family had prayed fervently to Therese Neumann, the finger instantly returned to normal sometime later as the boy was receiving Holy Communion. Another cure was that of a medical doctor who was suddenly cured of terminal lung cancer.

It is interesting to know that many requests to open the beatification research have also included the desire that the grave of Therese Neumann be opened before the beatification process begins. It is the belief of many people I have interrogated, and it is my own strong belief as well, that the body will be found exactly as it was when Therese lay in state before her burial.

During my most recent trip to Konnersreuth, which took place in May of 1985, I was able to visit with Father Anton Vogl (as well as with the two vice-postulators); Father Vogl told us about plans for the translation of Therese Neumann's body from the cemetery to the parish church. He explained that, under his direction, St. Lawrence parish is planning a crypt under the left side altar, the altar of St. Therese the Little Flower. It is well known that Therese Neumann wished eventually to be buried permanently under this side altar. Father Vogl kindly volunteered to explain the plan to me and the people in my group. I had never heard of this plan before, and I listened intently to what he had to say.

When the time comes that the body of Therese is actually exhumed from the cemetery and finally laid to rest in the crypt, it can be assumed that problems will arise because of all the people, buses and cars which can be expected—and which are already coming now. Surely this will create unnecessary noise for the faithful who are attending church services in their own parish. Therefore, plans have to be made now in order to alleviate problems before they are at hand.

Father Vogl gave us his version of what is planned. There is a small alley between the left side of the church and the old school building. The school building will eventually have to be torn down, and a crypt with an outside entrance will be built. This will enable the many visitors to view the tomb of Therese Neumann without interrupting services that might be in progress upstairs.

Recently (December 1986) I received word of some additional planned construction. Under orders from the Bishop of Regensburg, the lower right-hand part of the Neumann family home (underneath Father Naber's former apartment) is to be reconstructed to form an archives to house all the documents, films, etc. relating to Therese's cause. Father Vogl reports that the building of this new archives is "an absolute necessity" before the opening of the process of beatification.

Mention should be made here of a small publication which the Carmelites of the Theresianum publish twice a year; it is called *Konnersreuther Nachrichten* (*Konnersreuth News*). The address is:

Anbetungskloster Theresianum
Arzberger Strasse 11,
8591 Konnersreuth
West Germany

I happen to have several issues of this pamphlet-sized newsletter, printed over a number of years. I see from them that the sisters are constantly publishing voluntary depositions of miraculous healings that have occurred after the afflicted had asked Therese for help. They usually publish about six or seven of these depositions in each edition, so I presume that over the years there must have been hundreds of cures and instances of assistance received by people all over the world. I am happy that these events are constantly being reported and that the reports come from people on a voluntary basis.

When we visited Therese's grave in 1973, I was amazed at the number of wooden plaques on the grave, each with an appropriate text of thanks for healing or help received. In May of 1983 we counted over 100 such plaques. In fact, there have been so very many of these acknowledgments that there is not room for all of them on the grave, so they are exchanged periodically.

To help spread the knowledge of Therese Neumann, especially among people in the United States, I give talks to various groups and organizations. Over the years I have given over 50 talks to Catholic organizations and parish groups, as well as about 40 in private homes. Most of these were in California, though a few were in other locations—notably a lecture in 1950 to a large group of pilgrims aboard the ocean liner *SS America* returning to the U.S. from France, and one in 1983 at the Theresianum in Konnersreuth.

I am happy to say that the earlier edition of this book (a smaller volume entitled *The Life and Death of Therese Neumann, Mystic and Stigmatist*, Vantage Press, 1978) was very well received by all three postulators—Father Vogl, Father Veh, and Father Sträter. I trust that this new edition will bring even more people to become friends of Therese Neumann.

It must be remembered that investigations leading up to beatification and canonization cost a lot of money. Thousands of documents, many films, etc., have to be properly evaluated by experts, and such expenses that are incurred must be borne by the general public. As far as I know, they cannot be paid for out of normal diocesan funds. Therefore, a large number of people from Germany and all over the world have contributed to the diocese of Regensburg for this purpose. I would urge all who are in favor of the cause of Therese Neumann, and who voluntarily want to help on behalf of her possible beatification, to help defray the cost of the investigations involved.

However, I want to state in a most emphatic manner that

no donations should be sent to *anyone* except to the following three places, all of which are approved by the diocese of Regensburg:

> Rt. Rev. Manfred Müller
> Most Rev. Bishop of Regensburg
> Niedermünster Gasse
> D 8400 Regensburg
> West Germany

> Emmeram H. Ritter
> Diocesan Official
> Schwarze Bären Strasse 2
> D 8400 Regensburg
> West Germany

> Konnersreuther Ring e.V. (Konnersreuth Circle)
> Kapuzienergasse 2
> 8078 Eichstätt
> West Germany

All contributions should be made out to the "Therese Neumann Fund."

The above address on "Schwarze Bären Strasse 2" is the address of the "Department for Beatification and Canonization Processes of the Bishop's Consistory of the Diocese of Regensburg." It is of interest to note that this diocese is currently working on another beatification in addition to researching Therese Neumann's life for possible beatification.

I would also urge all friends of Therese Neumann and Konnersreuth to join the "Friends of the Konnersreuth Circle"; the offering is only $10.00 per year. Members receive a newsletter—usually once or twice a year, and more often if something very extraordinary occurs. All literature for the English-speaking world is being sent out in English through the good offices of: Mrs. Helga Rincker, who is also the secretary of Father Veh. Her address is:

Mrs. Helga Rincker
Franz Strasse 38
D 5800 Hagen I
West Germany

The Konnersreuth Circle, as a *pia unio,* has assumed the
role of executive body for the hoped-for beatification process
of Therese Neumann, with all the obligations arising out of
it, not the least of which is financial. This association also
strives to make Therese Neumann's life known through lectures, distribution of literature, and other means. Members
of the Konnersreuth Circle include Bishop Rudolf Gräber,
Father Anton Vogl (present parish priest of Konnersreuth),
Dr. Johannes Steiner (author of books on Therese Neumann),
one of Therese's brothers, and Father Ulrich Veh, O.F.M. Cap.

I have spoken to many people, and happily to many members of the clergy, who have written to the Bishop of Regensburg to have the beatification process opened as soon as
possible. If Cardinal Bea were alive today, he would surely
be in the forefront of such a move.

On the last page of this chapter I will give the friends
of Therese Neumann a convenient cut-out form requesting
the opening of her cause for beatification. This form was
prepared from a similar request circulated in the Catholic
community in Bavaria. It is self-explanatory and should be
properly signed.

To date, well over 13,000 requests for the beatification of
Therese Neumann have been received and processed by the
diocese of Regensburg. These have come from numerous European countries, as well as from the United States, Africa,
South America, Asia, and from behind the Iron Curtain. (This
information comes from the official *Positiones et Artikuli.)*

We, the friends of Therese Neumann, are now praying and
urging the Bishop of Regensburg to open the cause for Therese
Neumann's beatification.

— *Appendix* —

FATHER INGBERT NAAB'S
OPEN LETTER TO HITLER

Originally published in the Newspaper Der Gerade Weg
*in 1932. Reprinted in 1979 by the Konnersreuth Circle with
the following introductory explanation.*

The TV film "Holocaust" and the ensuing accusation against
the Roman Catholic Church that she had failed prompted us
of the "Konnersreuther Ring" to publish one of the many documents in our possession. It is one that found the most diffused
circulation in the fight against Hitler (20 million were printed!)
and was published in the paper *Der Gerade Weg* of March
20, 1932. It is an "Open Letter" by Fr. Ingbert Naab addressed
to Adolf Hitler. *Der Gerade Weg* had been fashioned within
the circle of friends around Therese Neumann as a paper that
stood against the fanatical spirit of evil of that time. Today
only Dr. Johannes Steiner, the then principal of the Nature
resp. Natural Law Publishing Firm that also published *Der
Gerade Weg,* is still living. The experienced journalist Dr. Fritz
Gerlich had found his way to the Roman Catholic Faith in
Konnersreuth and took upon himself the responsibility for the
often quite caustic tone of his paper. Once, when Dr. Gerlich
sharply pilloried certain measures of [Chancellor] Brüning,
he was restrained by Therese Neumann: "Brüning is quite all
right. He has made mistakes, but you, too, would have made
mistakes!" In this circle one valued a frank opinion.

Dr. Fritz Gerlich also claimed sole responsibility when he
was arrested. In 1934 he was one of the earliest victims in
the Dachau concentration camp. The Konnersreuth Circle not
only wishes to contribute to it that the fight against Hitler

161

is judged correctly, but their reprint from the time of battle without regard for personal safety ought to awaken people's consciences also in our present days. Fanaticism = terrorists, misled youth, derision of all Christian (not only Roman Catholic) principles, abortion = holocaust today, etc. afford an actual significance to the Capuchin Father's appeal to the conscience. *Der Gerade Weg* is being hushed up, one reason being that by recognizing the paper one would have to give Therese Neumann her rightful place! It will be seen that she is involved in the fight against fanatics and hysterics.

Fr. Ingbert Naab was himself a charismatic personality. He had to flee from place to place and was only just able to reach foreign soil. Therese Neumann visited him in Switzerland [where he died in 1935]. His body, now brought home, rests in the Capuchin cemetery at Eichstätt. Once open resistance was no longer possible, Konnersreuth became a token of support and hope, and that not only for Roman Catholics.

Superstitious fear prevented Hitler from removing Therese Neumann herself. But we recall the fate of the Konnersreuth school teacher Böhm, imprisoned by Nazis and hysterics in order to distress Fr. Naber and Therese Neumann. We recall the anguish of the Neumann family and all the inhabitants of Konnersreuth when the "SS" cannonaded Konnersreuth in 1945 since Therese herself could not be gotten rid of.

One comment cannot be offered: Fr. Ingbert has not attacked Protestantism, he merely stated that the then still prevailing antagonism against Roman Catholics drove many people into Hitler's camp.

In the General Election of March 13, 1932 that prompted Fr. Ingbert to write his appeal, [President] Hindenburg had just once more been victorious over Hitler.

The "Konnersreuther Ring" aims to distribute documents wherever possible; therefore, the "Open Letter" will be printed in its entirety.

Eichstätt, 20 March, 1979
Fr. Ulrich Veh, O.F.M. Cap.
Konnersreuther Ring

FR. INGBERT NAAB TO ADOLF HITLER
The well-known cleric reminds Adolf Hitler
with deep seriousness to remember his conscience and God.

Who has voted for Hitler? People with anti-Roman tendencies. A goodly number of misled idealists. The masses overpowered by suggestion. Those economically foundering. The cowards, position hunters and future party-book civil servants. Those people who are trying to escape from their financial responsibilities. The revolutionaries. A mass of unripe young people. The underworld of murder and intimidation of fellow men.

Dear Mr. Hitler,

It is not my profession to make politics and I do not have political intentions in writing this letter. But your political activities have one side that is deeply intruding into the conscience, into responsibility before God. These lines are meant to remind you of that.

When you were staying, guarded by 20 "SA" men, at the "Waldschlösschen" here at Eichstätt for the night of 13-14 March in order to confer with a friend of your organization, you arrived tired and rushed by your strenuous speech-tour, and doubly tired and beaten by the outcome of the election. There was no necessity to be guarded here, because in our "black" town nobody will harm you, even though your press coined a certain slanderous phrase: "black-red murder bunch." The townspeople said: "Hitler is on the run." You were not on the run, because nobody hunted you. In the morning in Munich you were able to issue your feeble proclamation without hindrance. Nevertheless, you are constantly on the run, on the run from your own conscience. You no longer allow yourself a quiet hour, and therefore your conscience is no longer able to make itself heard. Without pause you are hustled all over Germany. Only with difficulty are you able to reach the location of your next oration. The physical powers are strained to the utmost, and naturally your appearance is one of exhaustion. Your nerves no longer allow a quiet examination of conscience.

You are surrounded by flattery wherever you go and the frenzy of enthusiasm surrounding you at your gatherings prevents you from having any thought about whether your work will pass muster before God; because you are of the opinion: Germany is on my side. Your newspapers idolize you to a sickening degree. You are dubbed the "Great Redeemer from Want." You are yourself convinced of this, ascribing to your one and only personality all the attributes necessary to rebuild Germany. In the future you will need nothing at all by which to set your course. Your will is meant to be the only maxim for Germany and your command the only signpost. Has your conscience at any time reminded you of what a degree of self-assessment this conviction represents? Who among your followers dares to destroy this belief? How many from among the ranks of your own movement are hoping for an influential post? Will all these climbers and future party-book civil servants ever be critical of you? Your whole entourage is one conscience-narcotic for you.

You have many violent, fanatical persons among your followers, also among your sub-commanders. You wished for the wildest fanaticism, as especially expressed in your book *Mein Kampf.* But this wild fanaticism is driving you into situations you yourself must shudder to behold. If ever you should be tempted to follow a sensible thought, your sub-commanders would come to present you with accomplished facts. Only one way is then left open for you: to ridicule your subordinates, or yourself. Since you don't want either, safeguarding the interests of your movement before the eyes of the public, you submit to the situation and allow yourself to be hustled on and on. Not your conscience will be able to say the last word, but the hurry.

How necessarily you do need some quiet days, nobody speaking to you but your conscience. Days where you yourself do not speak, not to the populace nor to individuals—for when you do speak to individual people, you speak just as if you had the masses before you—

and where you yourself are not spoken to. Then your conscience could come into its own.

You and your press are stating: "The Future Germany," "The Elite of the Nation." There are indeed quite a number of idealists within your ranks who earnestly hope for everything good from you. These idealists do not know the true National Socialism, do not know what you are planning nor what you personally, or your agents, have negotiated. Could you risk showing your cards? You know, you would be stoned by the masses. You have indeed accused the Minister of Defence that the whole of Germany knew about your program except himself. But do be honest: does the mass of your adherers really know about your true program? Do not your papers proclaim loudly: "At first we just want to get to power; what we then do with this power remains to be seen." You have instilled such blind trust in your personality into the idealists that they see you as a God-given prophet to whose mission one has to submit. Seldom has a human being demanded so much servility of spirit as yourself, the "Herald of German Freedom."

Who has voted for you? People with anti-Roman Catholic tendencies! You have been baptized and raised within the Roman Catholic Church. One has never heard of you formally seceding from the Church. One of your Members of Parliament has in fact stated in the Berlin Sport Stadium that anyone maintaining you to be a R. Catholic was a common liar and a blackguard. No one familiar with your train of thought and your actions will assume you to have remained true to the Faith of your Church. You have never repudiated Arthur Dinter's statement giving your disclosure that the R. Catholic Church would have nothing to laugh about once you were in power. Your leanings are known, and therefore certain Protestant circles place all their hopes in you. When you observe the distribution of election results on a map, you will clearly notice that it is the Protestant areas who see you as their candidate, at least as regards the middle classes. The working class had rejected you. Protestantism leaves the Socialist working class cold; this aspect does not matter to them. Your future, Mr. Hitler, lies in the North. Certainly, there were some R. Catholics who gave you their vote. But they are Catholics who look upon themselves with peculiar feelings, obviously not seeing in what direction they are drifting. Men like Rosenberg [author of the official party line] and Stark could surely enlighten the Catholics. Mr. Goebbels [Minister of Propaganda], too, living in excommunication—as you well know, having been one of his marriage witnesses—could open the eyes of these Catholics. Mr. Hitler, speaking between ourselves: what do you think of the Catholics who voted for you? Blind herd or voters, what? You smile endorsement. I do not remind you that it would be an extremely serious question of conscience that you should ask yourself sometimes, being a Catholic, baptized but at variance with the Faith of the Church: can I justify myself before my God? But you may settle that with Him who will judge you.

Who has voted for you? The suggestible masses. You wished for mass-suggestion, talked about the necessity to force a foreign will on the masses, of rendering them fanatical and hysterical. You have been in this business now for more than 10 years. Your press is attuned solely to suggestion. Claims are made over and over until one feels quite stupid and dull. Again and again facts are suppressed, lie after lie is printed. Are you not responsible for this method? Propaganda, too, knows the laws of conscience.

Who has voted for you? Those economically foundering. They hope for deliverance through you. The farmer facing Public Sale, the businessman seeing no way out. "It can't get any worse," they say, "for 7 years now Hindenburg has been at the helm and achieved nothing. Now we'll give Hitler a chance, and if he is no good either we'll get rid of him." The psychology of those facing ruin is like that, Mr. Hitler. Your election is for many the least desperate measure, but not the last! There remains Bolshevism.

Who has voted for you? Those people who due to suggestion believed in the inevitability of you becoming President. "He'll come anyway," they said. And now one hears from many of them: "I'll no longer vote for him, I don't want to be ridiculed anymore." What an atmosphere on Monday! Mr. Hitler! Your masses who believed in the absolute victory were stunned. They hardly dared to look one in the face. They furtively passed their differently opinioned acquaintances. It went through a great many people, who had been perturbed and ready to submit to the inevitable, like a reviving breath of air. "It could still turn out differently," they said, relieved. The stupor began to lift.

Who has voted for you? The cowards who didn't want to lose their positions. Many people had already accommodated themselves to your rule, especially among those in state employment. For weeks they had hardly dared to do anything that could be considered hostile or unfriendly towards your party. After all, they wanted to keep their positions if Hitler should gain power. Mr. Hitler, what a cowardly company you raised with your dog-whip and the threats of your press! I congratulate you to these "Free German Men of the Third Reich." What do you yourself think of these people? Don't you have to say three times "For shame!" to each one?

Who has voted for you? Position hunters and future party-book civil servants. Have you ever considered how many among your people are counting on getting a safe employment on the basis of their enthusiasm for your person? How many were fool enough to think the 14th of March would produce the guarantee for their social security? Whilst on a train on 14th March I listened to the conversation of railway workers who were obviously Socialists. How these people mocked the disappointment of their National-Socialist friends: "Nothing doing with district manager! Go on shoveling coals!" one hailed a passer-by through the window. Mr. Hitler, who has thundered more against party bosses and party-book civil servants than yourself and your press, and who, more than you, has attracted a mass of people more sold on hopefully exclusive party protection? When you take over, then with you solely people of your own persuasion. You assert that again and again! Now then!

Will you ever again risk talking about party-book civil servants and party bosses when the whole structure of your state-to-be rests on just that? Where is your conscience in that? Mr. Hitler, there are grammar school pupils who have already pensioned off their grammars because they think their party loyalty will secure a position in the coming state even without a grammar. "Until Monday in the Third Reich!" was the farewell of such promising youths on the Saturday before the election. Would you call that sense of duty, or rather corruption of the worst kind? Mr. Hitler, your conscience will provide the answer.

Who has voted for you? People trying to escape their financial responsibilities. How many examples have come to my notice! There were people who defied their creditors with the message: "I don't pay anymore. Hitler is coming now and then I don't have to pay anything." Do you know of such practices? Has your party-till counted on the fact that March 14th would recognize the altered circumstances and legislation would soon wipe away old liabilities? But have you also considered the decline of morals passed on to the masses by these dubious speculations in a "Third Reich"? Are these dishonest persons, who care nothing for property and legal liability, really guarantors for Germany's ascent? Doesn't it rather smack of Bolshevism? And you are equally responsible with the others!

Who has voted for you? A mass of unripe young people. You pronounced that no one should dabble in politics before the age of 30 years, and now you know nothing more important than to get just these unripe youngsters into harness. What do you think about yourself and the honesty of your principles?

Who has voted for you? Revolutionaries. There are masses simply waiting to hit out, to destroy and plunder. You are for these persons the man who will give the signal to start the onslaught. That's why they give you their vote, they don't care what happens if only the action starts.

Who has voted for you? The underworld of murder and intimidation of fellow-men. The phrase is crass but only too true. You know yourself how those who don't conform are threatened by your own ranks. The gallows is a matter of course in the vocabulary of many of your followers. When someone does not know where to turn next, one says: "Wait, in the Third Reich there will be vengeance!" Isn't it yourself who sets this stone rolling? Wasn't the phrase: "Heads will roll!" the prelude to all these brutal intimidations? And this gangsterism reaches down to the phalanges of boys who know as much about politics as a calf does about science. In our peaceful Eichstätt the Cathedral Provost Wohlmut went one day to celebrate Mass in the Cathedral. A group of boys stood at the sacristy door; all greeted him except one. The sexton asked him, "Why don't you greet him?" And the answer? "I'm not greeting that one! He'll be shot when we are in power!" Who this boy is you may learn from any of your friends at Eichstätt. Do you know the name for such incitement? Is your conscience able to bear this corruption of the youth?

How Then Do You Mean To Go On?

I do not remonstrate on the political aspects, I leave that to those called to such things. I am appealing solely to your conscience. What do you say to the lie-propaganda? You had to have your attention drawn to the fact that your party promises all things to all men, even the most contradictory things. And why? What else but the lust for power. Do you think the Almighty will suspend the Eighth Commandment for your sake? "Lying lips are an abomination before the Lord" [*Prov.* 12:22] in the service of politics, too! And "lies are shortlived," even when spoken by eloquent men. Why don't you come into the open? Isn't your reticence in religious questions one great deception of the masses? Surely you yourself can only laugh about your program for a "Creed of Positive Christianity," otherwise you would not have a Rosenberg at your side. Doesn't your behavior in the question of religion strike even you as an intentional deception? How much longer do you intend to continue with it?

What do you say to the propaganda of hate? Your

principal paper, *Der Völkische Beobachter,* published in this week's Wednesday edition (Nr. 76, p. 3) an article by Gunter d'Alquen: "The fight goes on." It stated: "To our love that gives sense to our labors, we now add hate, hate for all that is against us. . .Our best troops are now thrown to the fore. We are going over to the offensive, there will be no prisoners taken, no further pardon given. We will advance; the tiniest shell-hole, the smallest shred of trench, all will be wiped clean, shattered, burnt out. We will pounce upon the enemy day and night, come rain or shine, we smite him wheresoever we meet him." That is the language of the insane. And "Positive Christianity"? A gospel of hate? Mr. Hitler, what does your conscience say?

Your Most Grievous Fault!

Mr. Hitler, the tearing apart of Germany, that is your fault, your conscience has to bear it. You want to unite the people? Do you consider these battle tactics suitable to unite a people? You could unite the people by exterminating all non-conformers, but not by any other means, at least not by you.

A possible civil war: that is your fault, your conscience has to bear it. You know you cannot grasp the helm legally in the near future. But your phalanges have been driven into such delusions that you are no longer able to keep them in a quiet mood. What will you do? Try to teach them reason? Then you are finished. Or drive them into further fantastic hopes? Your proclamation foreshadows that. You will then have to shoulder also all the results of these insane suggestions. Is your conscience able to bear that? Have you no fear that the dead will rise up against you to accuse you unceasingly during the lonely nights?

Despoilment of the youth: that is your fault, your conscience has to bear it. What you have sinned against the youth during the years of your influence, you will not easily wipe out. How often do we priests hear lamenting mothers say: "I can no longer make my son go to church. He thinks because he is a Hitler, he doesn't need our Lord God anymore." And how radical will this youth indoctrinated by your ideas become when they find themselves betrayed? You know it yourself: from your ranks to Bolshevism is but a step. For many the mental attitude is already the same. Prior to March 13th one heard from many of your people exactly the same slogans as at the time of the revolution [in 1914]. The lowliest employees have allocated all the posts—in readiness for March 14th, as if they had all commerce and civil servants' posts at their disposal. It is true, you are not responsible for every slogan uttered, but you are able to recognize the fruits of your labors.

The confusion of moral principles: that is your fault, your conscience has to bear it. The "Boxheim Documents" are becoming a precedent. There are many who would like to arrange themselves accordingly rather now than later. And your followers are supposed to be the "Cream of German Lands"? Thank you very much! But you are so modest when you claim that!

I have not touched upon the purely political side of the situation that ought to be discussed. For your conscience, that which I have said may be sufficient. We are preaching not the gospel of hate but of love, towards you too. Love contains above all our duty to tell you the truth, however bitter. We do not hold with lies, and refute them just as sharply when used against you as when damaging someone else. But you must not expect us to emphasize the Divine Commandments any less when they are inconvenient for the Third Reich.

Mr. Hitler, do not forget your conscience! And when you have examined it, then stand up and face Germany and make your great confession of guilt as you recognize it before God, from whom nothing is hidden. Your followers published a pamphlet in Munich, reciting for March 13th the Psalm, "Judge me, God, and take up my cause against an unholy people. From the treacherous and cunning man rescue me!"

We recommend this verse of the Psalm as a daily morning and evening prayer. But ask yourself first where this unholy people is, and who is the treacherous and cunning man. When studying for the priesthood we were admonished to look at ourselves as often as we recited this verse during Holy Mass, so that the Almighty might clean us of all self-deceit and injustice. It can only benefit you to give way to the same considerations.

Fr. Ingbert Naab, O.F.M. Cap.

Rt. Rev. Manfred Müller
Most Rev. Bishop of Regensburg
Niedermünster Gasse
84 Regensburg
West Germany

Subject: *Request to open the cause for the beatification of Therese Neumann.*

The undersigned is (are) convinced that the stigmatist Therese Neumann of Konnersreuth was in an extraordinary degree favored by the grace of God, and that by her heroic sufferings in expiation for sin, her charitable works for all classes of people, and through her life of prayer, she has proven herself worthy of being honored. Therefore, I (we) beg the favor that the present Most Reverend Bishop of Regensburg, as the competent authority, open the Diocesan Process for the Beatification of Therese Neumann.

Your humble and obedient servant(s) in Jesus Christ,

Name

Age

Occupation

Street

City, State, Zip

Amount of donation enclosed for Therese Neumann Fund (optional)

— *Data may be completed on back.* —

***If you have enjoyed this book, consider making your next selection
from among the following . . .***

Christian Perfection and Contemplation. *Garrigou-Lagrange, O.P.* 21.00
Practical Commentary on Holy Scripture. *Bishop Knecht.* 40.00
The Ways of Mental Prayer. *Dom Vitalis Lehodey* 16.50
The 33 Doctors of the Church. *Fr. Christopher Rengers, O.F.M. Cap.* 33.00
Pope Pius VII. *Prof. Robin Anderson* 16.50
Life Everlasting. *Garrigou-Lagrange, O.P.* 16.50
Mother of the Saviour/Our Int. Life. *Garrigou-Lagrange, O.P..* 16.50
Three Ages/Int. Life. *Garrigou-Lagrange, O.P. 2 vol.* 48.00
Ven. Francisco Marto of Fatima. *Cirrincione,* comp. 2.50
Ven. Jacinta Marto of Fatima. *Cirrincione* 3.00
St. Philomena—The Wonder-Worker. *O'Sullivan* 9.00
The Facts About Luther. *Msgr. Patrick O'Hare* 18.50
Little Catechism of the Curé of Ars. *St. John Vianney.* 8.00
The Curé of Ars—Patron Saint of Parish Priests. *Fr. B. O'Brien* 7.50
Saint Teresa of Avila. *William Thomas Walsh* 24.00
Isabella of Spain: The Last Crusader. *William Thomas Walsh* 24.00
Characters of the Inquisition. *William Thomas Walsh* 16.50
Blood-Drenched Altars—Cath. Comment. on Hist. Mexico. *Kelley* 21.50
The Four Last Things—Death, Judgment, Hell, Heaven. *Fr. von Cochem* ... 9.00
Confession of a Roman Catholic. *Paul Whitcomb* 2.50
The Catholic Church Has the Answer. *Paul Whitcomb* 2.50
The Sinner's Guide. *Ven. Louis of Granada* 15.00
True Devotion to Mary. *St. Louis De Montfort* 9.00
Life of St. Anthony Mary Claret. *Fanchón Royer* 16.50
Autobiography of St. Anthony Mary Claret. 13.00
I Wait for You. *Sr. Josefa Menendez* 1.50
Words of Love. *Menendez, Betrone, Mary of the Trinity.* 8.00
Little Lives of the Great Saints. *John O'Kane Murray* 20.00
Prayer—The Key to Salvation. *Fr. Michael Müller.* 9.00
Passion of Jesus and Its Hidden Meaning. *Fr. Groenings, S.J.* 15.00
The Victories of the Martyrs. *St. Alphonsus Liguori* 13.50
Canons and Decrees of the Council of Trent. *Transl. Schroeder* 16.50
Sermons of St. Alphonsus Liguori for Every Sunday. 18.50
A Catechism of Modernism. *Fr. J. B. Lemius* 7.50
Alexandrina—The Agony and the Glory. *Johnston.* 7.00
Life of Blessed Margaret of Castello. *Fr. William Bonniwell* 9.00
Catechism of Mental Prayer. *Simler* 3.00
St. Francis of Paola. *Simi and Segreti.* 9.00
St. Martin de Porres. *Giuliana Cavallini.* 15.00
The Story of the Church. *Johnson, Hannan, Dominica.* 22.50
Hell Quizzes. *Radio Replies Press* 2.50
Purgatory Quizzes. *Radio Replies Press* 2.50
Virgin and Statue Worship Quizzes. *Radio Replies Press* 2.50
Meditation Prayer on Mary Immaculate. *Padre Pio* 2.50
Little Book of the Work of Infinite Love. *de la Touche* 3.50
Textual Concordance of The Holy Scriptures. *Williams. pb.* 35.00
Douay-Rheims Bible. *Hardbound* 55.00
The Way of Divine Love. *Sister Josefa Menendez* 21.00
The Way of Divine Love. (pocket, unabr.). *Menendez* 12.50
Mystical City of God—Abridged. *Ven. Mary of Agreda* 21.00

Prices subject to change.

Visits to the Blessed Sacrament. *St. Alphonsus* 5.00
Moments Divine—Before the Blessed Sacrament. *Reuter* 10.00
Miraculous Images of Our Lady. *Cruz* 21.50
Miraculous Images of Our Lord. *Cruz* 16.50
Raised from the Dead. *Fr. Hebert*. 18.50
Love and Service of God, Infinite Love. *Mother Louise Margaret* 15.00
Life and Work of Mother Louise Margaret. *Fr. O'Connell* 15.00
Autobiography of St. Margaret Mary. 7.50
Thoughts and Sayings of St. Margaret Mary 6.00
The Voice of the Saints. *Comp. by Francis Johnston* 8.00
The 12 Steps to Holiness and Salvation. *St. Alphonsus*. 9.00
The Rosary and the Crisis of Faith. *Cirrincione & Nelson* 2.00
Sin and Its Consequences. *Cardinal Manning* 9.00
St. Francis of Paola. *Simi & Segreti* 9.00
Dialogue of St. Catherine of Siena. *Transl. Algar Thorold* 12.50
Catholic Answer to Jehovah's Witnesses. *D'Angelo* 13.50
Twelve Promises of the Sacred Heart. (100 cards). 5.00
Life of St. Aloysius Gonzaga. *Fr. Meschler* 13.00
The Love of Mary. *D. Roberto*. 9.00
Begone Satan. *Fr. Vogl*. 4.00
The Prophets and Our Times. *Fr. R. G. Culleton* 15.00
St. Therese, The Little Flower. *John Beevers* 7.50
St. Joseph of Copertino. *Fr. Angelo Pastrovicchi* 8.00
Mary, The Second Eve. *Cardinal Newman*. 4.00
Devotion to Infant Jesus of Prague. *Booklet* 1.50
Reign of Christ the King in Public & Private Life. *Davies* 2.00
The Wonder of Guadalupe. *Francis Johnston*. 9.00
Apologetics. *Msgr. Paul Glenn*. 12.50
Baltimore Catechism No. 1. .... 5.00
Baltimore Catechism No. 2. .... 7.00
Baltimore Catechism No. 3. .... 11.00
An Explanation of the Baltimore Catechism. *Fr. Kinkead*. 18.00
Bethlehem. *Fr. Faber*. 20.00
Bible History. *Schuster*. 16.50
Blessed Eucharist. *Fr. Mueller* 10.00
Catholic Catechism. *Fr. Faerber* 9.00
The Devil. *Fr. Delaporte* 8.50
Dogmatic Theology for the Laity. *Fr. Premm*. 21.50
Evidence of Satan in the Modern World. *Cristiani* 14.00
Fifteen Promises of Mary. (100 cards). 5.00
Life of Anne Catherine Emmerich. 2 vols. *Schmoeger* 48.00
Life of the Blessed Virgin Mary. *Emmerich* 18.00
Manual of Practical Devotion to St. Joseph. *Patrignani* 17.50
Prayer to St. Michael. (100 leaflets) 5.00
Prayerbook of Favorite Litanies. *Fr. Hebert* 12.50
Preparation for Death. (Abridged). *St. Alphonsus* 12.00
Purgatory Explained. *Schouppe* 16.50
Purgatory Explained. (pocket, unabr.). *Schouppe* 12.00
Fundamentals of Catholic Dogma. *Ludwig Ott*. 27.50
Spiritual Conferences. *Faber* 18.00
Trustful Surrender to Divine Providence. *Bl. Claude* 7.00
Wife, Mother and Mystic. *Bessieres*. 10.00
The Agony of Jesus. *Padre Pio* 3.00

Prices subject to change.

Seven Capital Sins. *Benedictine Sisters* 3.00
Confession—Its Fruitful Practice. *Ben. Srs.* 3.00
Sermons of the Curé of Ars. *Vianney* 15.00
St. Antony of the Desert. *St. Athanasius* 7.00
Is It a Saint's Name? *Fr. William Dunne* 3.00
St. Pius V—His Life, Times, Miracles. *Anderson* 7.00
Who Is Therese Neumann? *Fr. Charles Carty* 3.50
Martyrs of the Coliseum. *Fr. O'Reilly* 21.00
Way of the Cross. *St. Alphonsus Liguori* 1.50
Way of the Cross. *Franciscan version* 1.50
How Christ Said the First Mass. *Fr. Meagher* 21.00
Too Busy for God? Think Again! *D'Angelo* 7.00
St. Bernadette Soubirous. *Trochu* 21.00
Pope Pius VII. *Anderson* 16.50
Treatise on the Love of God. 1 Vol. *de Sales. Mackey, Trans.* 27.50
Confession Quizzes. *Radio Replies Press* 2.50
St. Philip Neri. *Fr. V. J. Matthews* 7.50
St. Louise de Marillac. *Sr. Vincent Regnault* 7.50
The Old World and America. *Rev. Philip Furlong* 21.00
Prophecy for Today. *Edward Connor* 7.50
The Book of Infinite Love. *Mother de la Touche* 7.50
Chats with Converts. *Fr. M. D. Forrest* 13.50
The Church Teaches. *Church Documents* 18.00
Conversation with Christ. *Peter T. Rohrbach* 12.50
Purgatory and Heaven. *J. P. Arendzen* 6.00
Liberalism Is a Sin. *Sarda y Salvany* 9.00
Spiritual Legacy of Sr. Mary of the Trinity. *van den Broek* 13.00
The Creator and the Creature. *Fr. Frederick Faber* 17.50
Radio Replies. 3 Vols. *Frs. Rumble and Carty* 48.00
Convert's Catechism of Catholic Doctrine. *Fr. Geiermann* 5.00
Incarnation, Birth, Infancy of Jesus Christ. *St. Alphonsus* 13.50
Light and Peace. *Fr. R. P. Quadrupani* 8.00
Dogmatic Canons & Decrees of Trent, Vat. I. *Documents* 11.00
The Evolution Hoax Exposed. *A. N. Field* 9.00
The Primitive Church. *Fr. D. I. Lanslots* 12.50
The Priest, the Man of God. *St. Joseph Cafasso* 16.00
Blessed Sacrament. *Fr. Frederick Faber* 20.00
Christ Denied. *Fr. Paul Wickens* 3.50
New Regulations on Indulgences. *Fr. Winfrid Herbst* 3.00
A Tour of the Summa. *Msgr. Paul Glenn* 22.50
Latin Grammar. *Scanlon and Scanlon* 18.00
A Brief Life of Christ. *Fr. Rumble* 3.50
Marriage Quizzes. *Radio Replies Press* 2.50
True Church Quizzes. *Radio Replies Press* 2.50
The Secret of the Rosary. *St. Louis De Montfort* 5.00
Mary, Mother of the Church. *Church Documents* 5.00
The Sacred Heart and the Priesthood. *de la Touche* 10.00
Revelations of St. Bridget. *St. Bridget of Sweden* 4.50
Magnificent Prayers. *St. Bridget of Sweden* 2.00
The Happiness of Heaven. *Fr. J. Boudreau* 10.00
St. Catherine Labouré of the Miraculous Medal. *Dirvin* 16.50
The Glories of Mary. *St. Alphonsus Liguori* 21.00
Three Conversions/Spiritual Life. *Garrigou-Lagrange, O.P.* 7.00

Prices subject to change.

Spiritual Life. *Fr. Adolphe Tanquerey*................................32.50
Freemasonry: Mankind's Hidden Enemy. *Bro. C. Madden*.............. 8.00
Fourteen Holy Helpers. *Hammer* 7.50
All About the Angels. *Fr. Paul O'Sullivan* 7.50
AA-1025: Memoirs of an Anti-Apostle. *Marie Carré.* 7.50
All for Jesus. *Fr. Frederick Faber.*............................16.50
Growth in Holiness. *Fr. Frederick Faber.*.......................18.00
Behind the Lodge Door. *Paul Fisher.*............................21.00
Chief Truths of the Faith. (Book I). *Fr. John Laux* 12.50
Mass and the Sacraments. (Book II). *Fr. John Laux* 12.50
Catholic Morality. (Book III). *Fr. John Laux.*.................12.50
Catholic Apologetics. (Book IV). *Fr. John Laux.*...............12.50
Introduction to the Bible. *Fr. John Laux*......................18.00
Church History. *Fr. John Laux*.................................27.50
Devotion for the Dying. *Mother Mary Potter*....................12.00
Devotion to the Sacred Heart. *Fr. Jean Croiset.*...............16.50
An Easy Way to Become a Saint. *Fr. Paul O'Sullivan* 7.00
The Golden Arrow. *Sr. Mary of St. Peter.*......................15.00
The Holy Man of Tours. *Dorothy Scallan.*.......................15.00
Hell—Plus How to Avoid Hell. *Fr. Schouppe/Nelson*..............15.00
History of Protestant Ref. in England & Ireland. *Cobbett*......21.00
Holy Will of God. *Fr. Leo Pyzalski* 7.50
How Christ Changed the World. *Msgr. Luigi Civardi* 9.00
How to Be Happy, How to Be Holy. *Fr. Paul O'Sullivan*.......... 9.00
Imitation of Christ. *Thomas à Kempis. (Challoner transl.)* 15.00
Life & Message of Sr. Mary of the Trinity. *Rev. Dubois*........ 12.00
Life Everlasting. *Fr. Garrigou-Lagrange, O.P.*.................16.50
Life of Mary as Seen by the Mystics. *Compiled by Raphael Brown* 15.00
Life of St. Dominic. *Mother Augusta Drane.*....................15.00
Life of St. Francis of Assisi. *St. Bonaventure* 12.50
Life of St. Ignatius Loyola. *Fr. Genelli.*.....................18.50
Life of St. Margaret Mary Alacoque. *Rt. Rev. Emile Bougaud* ...15.00
Mexican Martyrdom. *Fr. Wilfrid Parsons*........................12.50
Children of Fatima. *Windeatt.* (Age 10 & up)...................11.00
Cure of Ars. *Windeatt.* (Age 10 & up) 13.00
The Little Flower. *Windeatt.* (Age 10 & up)....................11.00
Patron of First Communicants. (Bl. Imelda). *Windeatt.* (Age 10 & up)...... 8.00
Miraculous Medal. *Windeatt.* (Age 10 & up) 9.00
St. Louis De Montfort. *Windeatt.* (Age 10 & up) 13.00
St. Thomas Aquinas. *Windeatt.* (Age 10 & up)................... 8.00
St. Catherine of Siena. *Windeatt.* (Age 10 & up) 7.00
St. Rose of Lima. *Windeatt.* (Age 10 & up) 10.00
St. Hyacinth of Poland. *Windeatt.* (Age 10 & up)..............13.00
St. Martin de Porres. *Windeatt.* (Age 10 & up)................10.00
Pauline Jaricot. *Windeatt.* (Age 10 & up) 15.00
Douay-Rheims New Testament. *Paperbound*.......................16.50
Prayers and Heavenly Promises. *Compiled by Joan Carroll Cruz*.......... 6.00
Preparation for Death. (Unabr., pocket). *St. Alphonsus*..............13.50
Rebuilding a Lost Faith. *John Stoddard* 16.50
The Spiritual Combat. *Dom Lorenzo Scupoli* 12.00
Retreat Companion for Priests. *Fr. Francis Havey* 9.00
Spiritual Doctrine of St. Cath. of Genoa. *Marabotto/St. Catherine* 12.50
The Soul of the Apostolate. *Dom Chautard* 12.50

Prices subject to change.

NOTES

NOTES

NOTES

NOTES

Adalbert (Albert) Vogl was born in 1910 in Altötting, Bavaria, West Germany. In 1923, at the age of 12, he emigrated to the United States, under the auspices of Father Joseph Steiger, settling down for a few years in Earling, Iowa, where he attended St. Joseph's parochial school. In 1927, after acquiring a fairly good command of the English language, he returned to his native Bavaria; it was at this time that he first met Therese Neumann, through his uncle, Msgr. Adalbert Vogl. Mr. Vogl became very militant in the fight against the Hitler party. As the danger increased, he was finally advised by Msgr. Adalbert Vogl to leave Germany; he did so, returning to Earling, Iowa in 1935 and becoming a United States citizen. (It was another of Mr. Vogl's uncles, Msgr. Karl Vogl, who wrote up the famous exorcism case which has been published as *Begone Satan*; Mr. Vogl had urged his uncle to write this story for publication in the German Catholic press.)

During World War II, as a member of the G-2 Section (Intelligence Dept.) of the Forward Headquarters of the U.S. Third Army under Gen. George Patton, Mr. Vogl had an opportunity to renew his acquaintance with Therese Neumann in Konnersreuth, Bavaria. He subsequently had other golden opportunities to visit with Therese, as well as with her pastor, Father Naber, Therese's father and other relatives, and with many priests, prelates and others who knew Therese well. Mr. Vogl is now retired. He lives in San Jose, California with his wife, Esther, who was also privileged to know Therese Neumann and who gave most valuable help in recording and organizing information on her. Mr. Vogl was one of the official witnesses called to testify in the investigative process of Therese Neumann; it is his great desire that she will soon be beatified.